Two things are needed in a good Christian book: principle and practice. The principles show the reader the reasons for doing something; the practice shows how to do it. There are plenty of books with much principle but little practice, so the reader never finds out how to do something. But Wendy's book is full of both principles that come from the Word of God and practices which have been born out of faithful application of those principles. I recommend this book heartily. The reader can trust what is found here. I would urge the reader to put into practice what is found in this book. They and those they minister to will be richly blessed.

Rev. Mike Flynn
Founder and Director, Fresh Wind Ministries
www.freshwindministries.org

> Mike served in the Episcopal Church as a parish priest for thirty years. Mentored by John Wimber in the 1980s, Mike and 1100 team members have led 150 conferences in the US and the Pacific Rim. He ministers internationally and has led Fresh Wind full-time since 1996.

Wendy Coy has given us a potent look at prayer! We all want to "Learn to Pray Like Jesus" but often we feel weak and empty... like a two-talent servant! This book will fill your tank and put ammo in your weapons of prayer! Read it with expectation and you won't be disappointed! Blessed are those who join Wendy in "Learning to Pray Like Jesus!"

Dr. Brian Simmons
Founder and Director, Apostolic Resource Center
www.thearcenter.org

D1499884

"Just tell us how," is the cry of most Christians. They have a desire to hear God's voice and put it into action. Wendy Coy gives us sound and practical steps to getting there. Wendy, along with her husband Phil, have years of experience helping the church understand how to "Hear God's Voice" and how to pray it forth. LEARNING TO PRAY LIKE JESUS in the hands of Christians can change a generation!

Todd Skeirik
Senior Pastor, Gateway Christian Fellowship, West Haven, CT
www.gateway-fellowship.org

Wendy Coy has done us a great favor. She has woven together in a wonderful way the teachings of Scripture on prayer, a lifetime of personal experience with prayer, and practicable wisdom. A threefold cord is not easily broken!

Using Jesus as a model for how we are to pray, she teaches us how to discern what God is doing, to put it into words, and to watch the prayers take effect. This is must reading for any who would want to pray with authority and minister effectively to the needs of others. There are a plethora of books with information about prayer, but here's a book that can change the way we pray.

Dr. Richard H. Jones

Dr. Jones served as a pastor in the Presbyterian Church (USA) for twenty-six years and now provides theological training for Christian leaders in the 10/40 Window.

Learning to Pray Like Jesus

John Five Nineteen

Learning to Pray Like Jesus

John Five Nineteen

Wendy Coy

The Two –Talent Series: Practical Ministry for the Rest of Us

ISBN: 978-0-9823721-3-5

Ascribe Publishing
38-11 Ditmars Blvd., Suite 595
Astoria, NY 11105
www.ascribepublishing.com

To Phil,

my love, my friend,
my partner in prayer,
my resident humorist
and wordsmith.

Thank you.

Forever.

Contents

Contents *(continued)*

Preface

Introducing the Two-Talent Series: Practical Ministry for the Rest of Us

> It will be like a man going on a journey who called his
> servants and entrusted his property to them. To one he gave
> five talents of money, to another two talents, and to another
> one talent, each according to his ability. Then he went on his
> journey. The man who had received the five talents went at
> once and put his money to work and gained five more. So
> also, the one with the two talents gained two more. But the
> man who had received the one talent went off, dug a hole in
> the ground and hid his master's money. After a long time the
> master of those servants returned and settled accounts with
> them. The man who had received the five talents brought the
> other five. "Master," he said, "you entrusted me with five
> talents. See, I have gained five more." His master replied,
> "Well done, good and faithful servant! You have been faithful
> with a few things; I will put you in charge of many things.
> Come and share your master's happiness!" The man with the
> two talents also came. "Master," he said, "you entrusted me
> with two talents; see, I have gained two more." His master
> replied, "Well done, good and faithful servant! You have been
> faithful with a few things; I will put you in charge of many
> things. Come and share your master's happiness!" (Matthew
> 25:14-23)

Two-talent Christians. We're the ones wondering how those
five-talent Christians do it. We gladly and faithfully invest
everything we have into the Kingdom of God. We've read
Matthew chapter 25 and we know that as we invest those two
talents, we will gain more. But those five-on-their-way-to-ten
talent Christians simply baffle us. We are *so* not them. They
have five children, home-school, start three businesses (which
are all successful), keep their cars immaculate and still have time
to run the Sunday School, go to board meetings, preach every
other Sunday and organize the prayer chain.

The rest of us, with our two talents, have uncounted piles of dirty laundry, can't find the can of Lysol, barely make it to work on time and end up at the drive-through for fast-food on the way to our small group. We can barely keep up with the prayer requests from our ten-talent brothers and sisters. We want to see great things happen, but we feel vastly unqualified.

Is there a place in ministry for us? We haven't studied theology, but we do pray. We don't want to be on stage, but we do want to see God move. We can't sing on pitch, but we love to worship. We can't preach sermons, but we do know our Scriptures. We pray and we want to be faithful.

Do we fit in anywhere? Can we learn to "do ministry?" Can God still use us with our two talents?

In a word, Yes. That's what this series is about. It's for those of us who don't "get it," but want to. This series is not esoteric, it's not complicated and it's not a religious formula. It's practical ministry for the rest of us, how-to's and stories for normal Christians.

...and the book

Learning to Pray Like Jesus: John Five Nineteen has been twenty-five years in the making. My husband Phil and I have prayed, learned, watched and ministered in thousands of settings, learning to pray effectively and "do what the Father is doing." (John 5:19) We're still learning. Our desire is to equip many more generations of Christians to hear the Father, do what He's doing, and minister daily to each other and the needy world around them. And they in turn will raise up more generations to do the same thing.

Over the course of those twenty-five years, we have learned from countless leaders, pastors, teachers and pray-ers. Each of them has unknowingly contributed to our unconscious database of stories, explanations, examples and beliefs. Much of our original understanding of the Kingdom of God and "doing what the Father is doing" was based on John Wimber's signs and wonders conferences in the mid 1980s. Still more of our understanding evolved from the early teaching of the Vineyard movement, and from Doug Gregg and Mike Flynn's prayer ministry training for Urbana ministry teams from 1990 to 2000.

Many other teachers and authors have affected us and deeply impacted our theology. Although the specifics of their lessons have long been forgotten, their stories and parables remain. We are so grateful for their teachings, ideas, illustrations and examples. Without their foundation our history would be quite incomplete.

Will you join us with your story? As we invest our combined talents, you'll be amazed how they grow!

Wendy (and Phil) Coy   October 2009

Introduction

This is a book of theology.

It's also a book of story.

And a book of practice.

Theology is the study of God. And every good theology is just a systematic putting together of the history (story) of what God has done. But every good story spells out a theology. It's the "who He is and why He does it" based on what we just saw Him do. We need to understand that our real theology is what we *actually* do and believe, not just what we *think* we do and believe. If we don't understand our real theology and how it needs to change, we'll do the practical things of life wrong. Every time. We'll act out of motives and beliefs we don't even know we have.

We have to know why we're doing what we're doing. That means we have to recognize and admit what we really do, and what we want to do, and recognize the difference. So we look at our stories, and we see what we actually have done and what it really means. And we see what God has done and how it has changed our theology. It does, you know. Seeing someone healed in Jesus' name, in front of your eyes, changes your theology of healing rather quickly. We look at our theologies. We study the Scripture and He changes our stories and our theologies to fit what He has already demonstrated.

And practice? Well, if we don't practice we won't learn how to do the "stuff" of stories – the stuff Jesus did, the stuff the disciples did and the stuff we can do, too. Healing. Hearing God. Doing what He is doing. We look at what He has said, what He has done. We change what we believe and we practice doing it. We practice so we're ready…

...Then He gives us more opportunities for stories: more chances to see Him heal, work, set free, love and change His people. The more we do, the more we learn and understand and the more we change.

There will be stories here; lots of them. Mine. Ours. Other people's. Also Scripture and a theology, an understanding of what God does and how and why (insofar as we can ever put God in a theological box. He always seems to jump out eventually when He does something we think is new).

We learn from these stories, from these theories, and we change. We recognize new boundaries to these fields we live in. The edges change, move, and are pushed farther back. There's suddenly more room to play, to grow, to minister, to enjoy Jesus, to be with each other. We venture into the new territory He's adding to the field we live in. It always surprises us, but if we keep listening and watching, we'll keep going safely and awesomely into these new places.

So this is an adventure, a story of going with the Lord, watching and doing all the things He does and learning what He is about. Of becoming effective, praying with authority and seeing Him work. It starts with some background, but then, of course, a story*...

---

*Names, locations and details have been changed in many stories throughout this book in order to protect the identity and privacy of those who received prayer. Some stories are compilations of several similar events used to illustrate the process of prayer.

The Beginning:
Changing Worldviews

Chapter One
One Verse

This is not how to start a book. You should start with a hook. Something intriguing. Something leading. Something engaging, and something that will keep the reader involved for the next few hundred pages.

Instead, I'm starting with a verse.

Just one verse. How can I base an entire approach, an entire ministry, on one verse? And why write a book with that one verse in its title?

Because it's a verse I've tried very hard to implement. I tried very hard for a very long time. I'm still working on it. It changed my life, and it may change yours.

> The Son can do nothing by himself; he can do only what he sees the Father doing, because whatever the Father does the Son also does. (John 5:19)

But, inevitably, one verse leads to another. The next verse repeats the thought (John 5:20) and later in John there's more:

> The words I say to you are not just my own. Rather, it is the Father, living in me, who is doing his work. Believe me when I say that I am in the Father and the Father is in me; or at least believe on the evidence of the miracles themselves. I tell you the truth, anyone who has faith in me will do what I have been doing. He will do even greater things than these, because I am going to the Father. And I will do whatever you ask in my name, so that the Son may bring glory to the Father. You may ask me for anything in my name, and I will do it. (John 14:10-14)

in the 80's. But this pastor obviously believed every ounce of that answer, even if it wasn't originally his.

Barely fifteen minutes earlier, he had stopped leading worship, hopped off the stage into the audience, prayed his way up the aisle, clambered over three rows of auditorium seating and made a bee-line directly to me. He obviously saw that God was doing something, something I felt but did not even begin to understand. He saw it, prayed for me, and I almost fainted. The Holy Spirit? Was that Him? I felt hot, flushed, tingly, and *seen* — somehow known and touched by Someone a lot bigger than the Jesus I was accustomed to. I knew that this prayer was for me, just me, among the hundreds in the high school auditorium.

This man read my heart, knew my thoughts, and prayed the only words that could have helped me. He didn't even know me; he'd never seen me before. How did he do it? How did he *know*? Did the look on my face give him answers to questions I didn't know I was asking?

My face. It had to be the look on my face. That was it, wasn't it?

No, that wasn't it. I sat down heavily, not wanting to leave that room, that moment, that sense of Jesus' presence where God was so obviously speaking, moving, working. What on earth – or in heaven – was going on? I didn't know, but I liked it. I wanted more. But more importantly, I wanted to do whatever this was.

My husband and I followed this praying man around for the next hour, watching and taking notes as he prayed for dozens of eager worship leaders. By the time the weekend was over, I learned about names and books I'd never heard of, concepts and Scriptures I'd never explored. I wrote fast. I could tell this was going to be a steep learning curve. But I was hooked, completely won over and convinced. Everything that he prayed was effective. Everyone he prayed for was touched, changed, healed, helped, and loved. I'd never seen so many tears—first of sorrow, then of joy—in one place. Whatever this was, it was God moving, and it was working.

I spent the next six months in a blur. By all outward appearances I lived my normal life. I led worship, made schedules, planned meetings, rehearsed, collected songs and led small groups. But I also went to conferences, prayed, worshipped, watched, and copied everything I saw that "worked." Jesus was breaking out, healing was happening, and every time I heard "Come, Holy Spirit," God would start to do something in me.

This was a new and different thing entirely. It wasn't just the presence of God. It was His people, coming alongside what God was doing, and praying effectively so that His presence was magnified and His work was accomplished. Every time, whether during worship or prayer, someone would see the "it" that God was doing and pray for me. And every time something new and strange happened. God's presence was so powerful I could barely stand on my own.

Slowly, I began to see what the praying pastor saw—God at work in front of me. The words that people prayed—THEIR words? GOD's words?—had effect. Apparently, the words they said were not just "their" words. That, in essence, was the key. They heard from God.

I needed to learn to hear from God in a new way, to understand what it was to watch God at work, to know what He was doing, to put it into words and see—actually see—the prayers take effect.

The worldview shift—God at work all around me, all the time, everywhere I went—happened fast.

Learning to listen differently did not.

I was excited, but I was intensely frustrated. No amount of learning seemed to break through my old mindset. What was it like to hear from God? *How* could I hear from God? How did all those effective pray-ers *do* it?

I had to find out. I couldn't go back to normal (boring) Christianity as I'd known it. This was life. It was effective, surprising, and wonderful. It was also hard, controversial, and life-changing. But I couldn't, and wouldn't, let it go.

Chapter Three
Intimacy

My journey had started a year-and-a-half before the conference at a prototypical small, white, New England evangelical church.

I walked into the church hallway for the first time to interview for the Minister of Music position. Someone was playing worship songs on the stage keyboard. In a flash, my legs were weak. God ambushed me. Again. I wanted to sit down, lie down, find a way to concentrate on Jesus. I wanted to bless Him, love Him, and just "be" with Him. I looked around. No chair in sight, and the pastor's door was about to open. I settled for a nearby wall and leaned heavily against it, hoping I would stay upright and not melt slowly into the floor. The presence of Jesus washed over me, taking me somewhere else. Somewhere else with Him.

Hearing a noise from the secretary's office, I groped for the door jamb. Focus, Wendy, focus. Pulling myself together, I wondered at how fast I'd gone from together-professional-job-interviewee to weak-kneed-swooning-lover-of-Jesus. The Spirit of God clearly was up to something. Here I was, an unintentional worship stowaway, riding the coattails of someone else's private adoration. I didn't even know the song or the person playing. And he, whoever he was, had no idea I was listening. What was the Lord doing in this little conservative church?

Two hours later I knew I had the position. So did the pastor, but we had to wait. We had to go through the proper channels. Voting. Unanimous approval from the elders, the deacons, the choir, the congregation, the pope… It was a long, arduous process. But I hardly noticed. I kept thinking about the worship. Clearly, the congregation was in for something fresh if this was the way worship was going to go.

Now, post-conference, and swirling in the cyclone of a brand-new worldview, we were thrust into a new realm. We weren't in Kansas anymore. For the next year the Holy Spirit wooed us and won us, showing us dimensions of intimacy that we hadn't known. The congregation didn't know it yet, but the fledgling worship team was completely smitten with the Presence of the Lord. We could play for hours, not even caring if we changed songs. It was a holy love affair, the Bridegroom romancing the Bride.

It began to change us. We wanted nothing more than to be with Jesus. Whatever He was doing, we wanted more. We worshipped to new songs, lots of them, especially songs of presence—"love songs to Jesus." And old songs, hymns, choruses, anything that addressed the Lord directly. We adored Him and sang those songs again and again. It was as if we understood intimacy with the Lord for the first time. It wasn't about the First Corinthians spiritual gifts. It wasn't about being "charismatic." It was just about Jesus.

Now I have all sorts of words for what happened, but in that season we just wanted to be in the presence of the Lord.

We didn't see it at the time. But we were changing. We had moved. We were no longer begging for Him to "do something." We were being loved by Jesus. We were becoming the Bride, the one whom Jesus died to win.

Chapter Four
Who Are We When We Pray?

Bride? Jesus' bride? Now that's an uncomfortable notion for most of us. "Child" we can handle. "Heir" is quite noble. But "bride?" The intimacy implied in that concept makes us squirm. And "Warrior?" Let's not even go there.

But Jesus *did* go there. He went there in our little evangelical church whether we were comfortable or not. Child... heir...warrior...bride. He was changing our whole notion of who we were. We thought we were worshippers, worship leaders, and pray-ers. We weren't used to this "bride" language.

He began to ask very uncomfortable questions: "Do you know Me intimately? Do you want to know Me more? Will you come closer, so we can talk? Will you go to new places where you haven't wanted to go?" This was a whole new ballgame.

Jesus didn't seem to be content with the way things had been. He wanted relationship. He wanted communion. He wanted intimacy. He wanted us to grapple with the deeper issue: who were we really when we stood in front of Him? A begging widow? A glorious bride? A warrior of freedom?

Our answers changed how we talked. They changed how we worshipped. And most of all, they changed how we prayed.

Now, as then, our answers determine what we hear from the King.

A Begging Widow

For many of us the practice of prayer is limited to intercession, when we cry out to God to meet the needs around us. We have understood our rights and privileges before the Father: that if we ask anything in His name, He will hear us in heaven. We have hope and boldness to persist in prayer. We pray, we pray often, and we pray until something happens. But our image of intercession is not always positive because we approach it wrongly.

Think of it this way: if you have a personal request for a Very Important Person who is Very Busy and has a Long Title on his door and Very Many Important Things to Do, you might cautiously go to his office. If invited, you might ask politely and wait for a response, but you don't really expect an intimate dialogue. Certainly, if you think he is not listening, you have two choices: speak louder and longer or go away. Going away will not produce the desired result; you won't get what you asked for. Talking louder and longer? That might bear results. Maybe.

Often we think that begging is our position before God. Unfortunately, we buttress this view by misapplying the Scripture about the widow:

> Then Jesus told his disciples a parable to show them that they should always pray and not give up. He said: "In a certain town there was a judge who neither feared God nor cared about men. And there was a widow in that town **who kept coming to him with the plea**, 'Grant me justice against my adversary.'
>
> For some time he refused. But finally he said to himself, 'Even though I don't fear God or care about men, yet because this widow keeps bothering me, **I will see that she gets justice, so that she won't eventually wear me out with her coming!**'"

And the Lord said, "Listen to what the unjust judge says. And **will not God bring about justice for his chosen ones,** who cry out to him day and night? Will he keep putting them off? I tell you, he will see that they get justice, and **quickly.** However, when the Son of Man comes, will he find faith on the earth? (Luke 18:1-8, emphasis mine)

We tend to think that this passage teaches us to badger and pester an unwilling God. Instead, Jesus shows us a Heavenly Father who loves us much more than does the unjust judge. Our Father will readily, eagerly hear us, and He will answer more quickly than the judge. The questions are whether we will choose to believe that He hears and answers and whether we will learn to trust Him. Too often we forget.

A Bride

Two other potent images of our position in prayer are more symbolic, but equally real. The Book of Esther and the Song of Songs (Song of Solomon) can be read as symbolic of our standing as the Beloved of the Lord. Each foreshadows our relationship with Jesus as the Lover of our souls, as well as our Savior and Lord.

Esther's bridal relationship with the King is secured by his love and by their marriage, but she is still the queen and must live by the accepted royal protocol: only those the King summons may see him. She knows that she risks her own life by going to the King unbidden, but she must make a request she hopes will save her people. Relying on his love, she presents a wine banquet, a reminder of his passion for her and their engagement. She is counting on his mercy.

His response is to grant her anything she desires: "Queen Esther, what is your petition? It will be given you. What is your request? Even up to half the kingdom, it will be granted." (Esther 5:3) Such is the love that our Father has for us that He wants to hear and respond to our needs. He wants to have conversation and relationship with us.[1]

In the Song of Songs we are allegorically the Bride, this time loved and pursued by the Lord who is also our Beloved. He responds to the Bride. He delights in her and she in Him. It is a compelling picture of lovers who will do anything for each other, eagerly outdoing one another in passion and giving.[2]

Surely, if we are that beloved bride, then we are loved and heard. The Bridegroom wants to speak, as well as listen.

What bride would marry a groom who demanded praise, worship, and adoration, and never spoke lovingly to his beloved? What loving husband would stand coolly by, listening and not responding to the adoration and requests of his bride?

Our relationship of love with Jesus was conceived from the beginning of time to be one of sharing and dialogue, passion and real relationship. Jesus desires us and wants to communicate with us, the Bride He died for, forever.

A Warrior

The bridal image is not the only way we view our relationship with the Lord. He is our love, but also our King and our Commander-in-Chief. As we will see later, we are a people at war, and although it may be an unpopular image in our culture, we are warriors in His army.

The battle, however, isn't exactly what we expect.

---

[1] For a more thorough treatment, see Gary Wiens, *Bridal Intercession, Authority in Prayer Through Intimacy With Jesus,* Oasis House, 2001.
[2] For an expansion of this allegory, see Brian Simmons, *Song of Songs, the Journey of the Bride.* Insight Publishing Group, 2002.

The ministry of Jesus begins an invasion: the Kingdom of God displacing the kingdom of Satan. We are clearly under orders and we are clearly in that battle.

The biblical writers were quite familiar with the language of battle, and they knew exactly what it would mean to their readers. For example:

> From the days of John the Baptist until now, the kingdom of heaven has been forcefully advancing, and forceful men lay hold of it. (Matthew 11:12)

> For though we live in the world, we do not **wage war** as the world does. **The weapons we fight with** are not the weapons of the world. On the contrary, they have **divine power to demolish strongholds**. We **demolish** arguments and every pretension that sets itself up against the knowledge of God, and **we take captive** every thought to make it obedient to Christ. (2 Corinthians 10:3-5)

> Finally, be strong in the Lord and in his mighty power. **Put on the full armor of God** so that you can take your stand against the devil's schemes. For **our struggle** is not against flesh and blood, but against the rulers, against the authorities, against the powers of this dark world and against the spiritual forces of evil in the heavenly realms. **Therefore put on the full armor of God**, so that when the day of evil comes, you may be able **to stand your ground**, and after you have done everything, to stand. (Ephesians 6:10-13, emphasis mine)

Our prayers have authority and impact because the Word of the Lord is our offensive weapon; we are on the offensive to take back what has been stolen.

But the way we fight looks more like a festival of love.

Armed with the salvation and love of Jesus and with faith, truth, righteousness, and peace (see Ephesians 6:14-17), we are called to restore birthrights to sons and daughters of God. We fight against evil and its effects in the world and in ourselves—by loving and healing.

This is more than just the traditional meaning of "spiritual warfare." Yes, we are to resist the enemy, and he will flee. Yes, we are to deliver the captives and set them free from the grasp of the enemy.

Deliverance is real and necessary, but no battle is won simply by fighting the negative. We bring the positive—salvation, truth, freedom and the love of God—to break the strongholds the enemy has built. We take the offensive by bringing His love to those around us. We heal the sick, raise the dead, love our neighbors and serve the poor. How powerful it is to bring love and light to drive out darkness.

To be carriers of that healing power and of His glory is our right, our opportunity, and it should be our passion. It is also our mandate for the battle. Our prayer is a potent weapon to win the war.

A Warrior Bride

The very feminine image of the bride seems incompatible with the masculine image of the warrior, yet the combination of the two brings a powerful balance to our prayer.

We intercede on behalf of our brothers and sisters, preparing the battleground. We receive and give the extravagant love of Jesus, poured out so generously in intimacy to His Bride; we take back the ground the enemy stole; we rescue the lost, broken, and weary (both in prayer and in service); and we stand our ground, releasing men and women into freedom and ministry as sons and daughters, heirs of the King and a Bride to His Son.

It is precisely the continuing cycle of receiving and giving love, healing and rescuing, loving and serving, equipping and empowering, that represents maturity in our relationship with Jesus. He gives us the love, the power, and the authority to bring freedom and healing as we pray.

As we listen to the Father's heart and respond actively, knowing that He desires to work through us, we no longer have to beg. Instead, we stand and act in His name, giving that which we have received, doing that which we hear, and watching people walk free, able to be who they were redeemed to be.

Does the thought that you are a Bride, even a Warrior Bride, and not a begging widow, change your attitude about who you are when you pray? Does it make you think that relationship—and even dialogue—is possible? After all, the Commander talks with his army and the Bridegroom with His Bride.

My standing as a Bride, and a Warrior Bride, gives me hope. It makes me eager to pursue a lover who can't wait to walk and talk with me, to reveal to me what He is doing, and to give me all the tools I need to see His purpose accomplished.

But first I—we—have to discover a new way of praying.

Chapter Five
Heartfelt Cry and Dialogue: The Challenge of Two-Way Thinking

David understood well that he had a relationship with the Living God. He knew both aspects of loving his King: he was strong and capable as a warrior for the Lord and passionate in his adoration and worship. He talked with God abundantly, honestly, and openly.

In the Psalms, David is hardly shy about his emotions and thoughts. Much of what he writes is almost embarrassingly real. He rejoices, gets angry, pleads, sings, cries, laments and demands vengeance. In fact, he goes further than most of us would dare. In Psalm 59, he is surrounded by Saul's army and he is not gentle, kind, or loving in his prayer:

> God will go before me and will let me gloat over those who slander me. But do not kill them, O Lord our shield, or my people will forget. **In your might make them wander about, and bring them down. For the sins of their mouths, for the words of their lips, let them be caught in their pride. For the curses and lies they utter consume them in wrath, consume them till they are no more.** Then it will be known to the ends of the earth that God rules over Jacob. They return at evening, snarling like dogs, and prowl about the city, they wander about for food and howl if not satisfied. But I will sing of your strength, in the morning I will sing of your love; for you are my fortress, my refuge in times of trouble. O my strength, I sing praise to you. You, O God, are my fortress, my loving God. (Psalm 59:10-17, emphasis mine)

I doubt that many pastors would be comfortable if we started praying this way. For that matter, *I* wouldn't be comfortable if *I* started praying this way, but at least David's prayer is not all vengeance.

David moves from anger and retribution to declaring the name and the love of the Lord. There is pure emotion here and a cry for help. It is gut level honesty. And that honesty allows David to move, finally, to a reliance on the Lord's strength and care.

This is real relationship. And it's the kind of communication the Father loves to hear. He delights in the honest emotion and passion of our hearts, released to the only One who can do something about it.

As powerful as this honesty is, and as freeing, God desires even more. He desires as close and open a relationship as any we see here on earth. He, the God of the Universe, desires to talk to us and dialogue with us and He invites our response. Our Creator wants to relate to us the way we would to our closest friend.

Holy Debate

The Old Testament is full of examples of the conversation that God wants with us. The patriarchs spoke freely with the Almighty and lived to tell about it. They spoke honestly to the Lord and He spoke honestly with them. In fact, on occasion they bargained.

Take Abraham for example. When God decided to obliterate Sodom and Gomorrah, Abraham resisted. He fought for his people and confronted God with His nature to be merciful and just. We join the scene as God is about to act:

> Then the LORD said, "The outcry against Sodom and Gomorrah is so great and their sin so grievous that I will go

down and see if what they have done is as bad as the outcry that has reached me. If not, I will know."

The men turned away and went toward Sodom, but Abraham remained standing before the LORD. Then Abraham approached him and said: "Will you sweep away the righteous with the wicked? What if there are fifty righteous people in the city? Will you really sweep it away and not spare the place for the sake of the fifty righteous people in it? Far be it from you to do such a thing—to kill the righteous with the wicked, treating the righteous and the wicked alike. Far be it from you! Will not the Judge of all the earth do right?"

The LORD said, "If I find fifty righteous people in the city of Sodom, I will spare the whole place for their sake."

Then Abraham spoke up again: "Now that I have been so bold as to speak to the Lord, though I am nothing but dust and ashes, what if the number of the righteous is five less than fifty? Will you destroy the whole city because of five people?"

"If I find forty-five there," He said, "I will not destroy it."

Once again he spoke to Him, "What if only forty are found there?"

He said, "For the sake of forty, I will not do it."

Then he said, "May the Lord not be angry, but let me speak. What if only thirty can be found there?"

He answered, "I will not do it if I find thirty there."

Abraham said, "Now that I have been so bold as to speak to the Lord, what if only twenty can be found there?"

He said, "For the sake of twenty, I will not destroy it."

Then he said, "May the Lord not be angry, but let me speak just once more. What if only ten can be found there?"

He answered, "For the sake of ten, I will not destroy it."

> When the LORD had finished speaking with Abraham, He left, and Abraham returned home. (Genesis 18:20-33)

This is not our normal mode of prayer! Note that it is Abraham who initiates this whole encounter—he stays standing before the Lord and speaks. It is also Abraham who stops bargaining with God, not the other way around. And God is not angry with him.

I must ask in the spirit of honest conversation why Abraham did not bargain all the way down to one. What would God have done? To be fair, the Scripture says, "When the Lord had finished speaking with Abraham, He left." So perhaps the Lord made it clear that enough was enough. But if we are going to converse this honestly with the Lord of the Universe, and live to talk about it, why should we not boldly ask as much as we can?

If I have any desire at all to ask questions when I reach Heaven, this will probably be one of the first. Abraham? Oh Abraham...? What were you thinking?

Of course, he is not the only one who debated.

Moses also famously bargained with God. As frustrated as he was with the people he led out of Egypt, Moses was not content to watch the Lord wipe them off the face of the earth. "It would not look good to the Egyptians," he argued, more or less. And his trump card? "Besides, You promised."

Oh, my. Would I have had the fortitude to challenge the Living God like that? Listen as the Lord reveals His frustration to his servant and friend Moses:

> "I have seen these people," the LORD said to Moses, "and they are a stiff-necked people. Now leave me alone so that my anger may burn against them and that I may destroy them. Then I will make you into a great nation."

But Moses sought the favor of the LORD his God. "O LORD," he said, "Why should your anger burn against your people, whom you brought out of Egypt with great power and a mighty hand? Why should the Egyptians say, 'It was with evil intent that he brought them out, to kill them in the mountains and to wipe them off the face of the earth'? Turn from your fierce anger; relent and do not bring disaster on your people."

"Remember your servants Abraham, Isaac and Israel, to whom you swore by your own self: 'I will make your descendants as numerous as the stars in the sky and I will give your descendants all this land I promised them, and it will be their inheritance forever.' " Then the LORD relented and did not bring on his people the disaster he had threatened. (Exodus 32:9-14)

Well, now. Moses and Abraham seem rather bold in their conversations with God. Either they are an exception, emboldened because of their calling and "special" relationship with God, or we are all invited to converse this freely with the Lord.

Just to get myself off the hook, I would rather opt for the former (their special-ness), but the entire body of Scripture argues against that. The vast majority of the great Old Testament figures were equally bold with the Lord. And Peter, James, John and a multitude of others talked with Jesus the same way in the New Testament.

To my chagrin, I am left to conclude that we are no different than they.

The Lord obviously delights in a Bride who will converse with Him freely and with whom He can have honest and real conversations. He is clearly eager to speak with her.

What about us? Are we willing to enter into such an honest dialogue with our Creator? Are we willing to hear His side in our prayer conversations? To debate, to love and to lament—all at the same time? Think carefully before you answer. Your entire prayer life hinges on your response.

Because...if He is so eager to speak, then we must learn to be honest in our response.

And we must learn to listen.

Doing What the Father is Doing:
Listening, Watching, and
Discerning

Chapter Six
Doing What the Father is Doing: Listening

Listening is hard. I don't like it. I concentrate mightily and I imagine in my mind what the other person is saying. I get it. But it takes all of my energy to concentrate and focus, leaving none for response. My ADD brain[3] simply can't work on more than one track at a time and focus is its nemesis.

Which is why I failed miserably at hearing God for the first several years. I tried so terribly hard, listening with my eyes squeezed shut, blocking out every thought and every noise, using every ounce of concentration I could muster. It didn't work very well.

What a relief to find out that's not how it's done. But we'll get to that soon. Let's start with some background first.

Remember, Jesus is our model. In everything we do we have to follow His example. That means we should pray like Him, minister like Him, teach like Him, heal like Him, and be like Him. And listen like Him. Listen? Did *He* listen? Did He show us how to listen?

Yes—and no. Let me explain.

Of course He listened. He just didn't explain what He did. Perhaps He didn't need to explain to his Judean audience. Perhaps Jesus' listening was implied, or obvious. But somehow,

---

[3] I have Attention Deficit Disorder; no derision is implied here. The disorder often enables my creativity, but it hinders my sense of organization, linear thinking, and focus.

He always knew what He had to do, what to say, where to go. How could He know as unerringly as He did? He must have listened well.

> One of those days Jesus went out to a mountainside to pray, and spent the night praying to God. When morning came, he called his disciples to him and chose twelve of them. (Luke 6:12-13)

It's a complete argument from silence but do you suppose that Jesus, during that long night on the mountain, prayed about whom to call as disciples? How do you suppose He heard the answer? He was, after all, just as human as we are. Did God speak to Him differently than He speaks to us? I suppose that's possible, but if God spoke differently and more easily to His Only Son, why did Jesus have to spend the whole night praying? Wouldn't the answers have come quickly to Him?

He never tells us—and the Scripture is uniquely quiet about the issue—whether He asked His Father what to do. Nor does He say whether He heard a response, nor even *how* He listened. But He knew what to do the next morning and He clearly had an answer from the Father.

That wasn't the only time, either. We see a pattern here. After healing and teaching, Jesus often went away—alone—to pray. Before the Transfiguration, he withdrew to pray. At Gethsemane, he prayed. Jesus was a man of prayer, a man who spent time with His Father, and a man who listened. Even at Gethsemane, Jesus pleaded with His Father to let Him take another way, if possible, but He proceeded to the cross with intention, clarity, and purpose. Again, He must have heard an answer.

Therefore we surmise that it is possible to hear from God. Certainly, the Scripture implies it. Jesus says clearly in John 10:27, "My sheep listen to my voice; I know them, and they follow me." John chapter 10 verses 3, 4 and 16 all speak about the sheep knowing (and listening for) the shepherd's voice. We already saw that the Old Testament is full of references to God and man (in the generic sense) speaking together. We just listened in as Abraham and Moses both debated with God — they must have heard and responded as if God were "right there." Today, such a testimony of direct dialogue with God would cause us to doubt the mental stability of the speaker.

Clearly, this is behavior that Jesus expects from us and He obviously does not expect it to be hard! Sheep, after all, are notoriously dumb animals, yet even *they* recognize the shepherd's voice. I've seen a sheep bleat raucously for the shepherd to come rescue him from a very shallow ditch. He obviously knew the shepherd when the shepherd showed up. I refer to real sheep, of course, but I suppose we can all think of examples of human "sheep" doing the same thing. (None of *us*, of course!)

Jesus knew what to do. He knew when to pronounce forgiveness of sins, when to put mud in someone's eyes or stick His fingers in their ears, when to tell them to wash, when to tell them to stand and walk, and when to command evil spirits to leave. He taught with authority and clearly knew information that other people didn't. The woman at the well wisely said "Sir, I perceive that you are a prophet…"

Let's return again to John 5:19: "The Son can do nothing by Himself; he can do only what He sees His Father doing…" Jesus didn't initiate ministry. He responded to the Father's actions. How? By being so in tune with His Father that He knew in the moment what to say and do. God showed Jesus what to do and Jesus did it. He wants us to do the same.

How Does God Speak? Prayer as a Dialogue with God

I didn't imagine it would be this hard. Everyone around me seemed to be able to hear from God. Everyone. All the pastors, all the leaders. They saw pictures. They dreamed dreams. They knew what to pray and their prayers consistently "worked." I mean, people were actually *healed* when these leaders prayed. Things happened. Meanwhile, I sat there wondering how to hear. I couldn't get started. I simply didn't "hear" anything.

The harder I tried (remember, I was squeezing my eyes shut and concentrating as hard as I could) the worse it got. The pastor would say, "All right, let's be quiet and just listen," confident that God would actually speak and tell us what to do. Even worse, people all around me, including my husband, seemed to "hear" from God, right at that moment. (What? Him too? I must be really weird. Defective. Doing something wrong.) I redoubled my efforts to "hear" and tried to stop my racing mind, which jumped with abandon, hither and yon, wandering at will, when all I wanted was for it to BE QUIET! (Sorry, did I just yell that? That's what it felt like inside.)

God, in His mercy, must have realized how close I was to shutting down every intuitive way of hearing from Him, for that is indeed what I was doing. He sent a wonderful adventure to help me.

Not long after I reacted to my "hearing deficiency," we were invited to visit a church that practiced a ministry of prayer. This was not a small ministry of prayer, but a large, multi-campus ministry that was building toward all-day and all-night, continuous worship and prayer. I was already praying in several groups, but I hadn't truly grasped the depth of what prayer as dialogue really was. I still struggled with what to pray, how to fit into the flow of prayer, and how to really "get it." I always felt like I prayed the wrong thing at the wrong time.

Sometime during that weekend visit, a leader talked about prayer as conversation with God. I realized for the first time that intercession was simply talking to Jesus as if He were in the room. Really? Just talking? As completely elementary as it sounds, I realized during that weekend that I'd had a deep prayer life for years, just not the three-hours-kneeling-by-the-side-of-the-bed-beseeching-heaven kind. I routinely walked around the house thinking in God's general direction. Sometimes I even ranted silently to Him, going on at great length about the issues that unsettled my heart, or the painful relationships which hurt my friends, or the situations that just needed God's help.

Suddenly, I realized that my silent rants were prayers.

The change in perspective was like the difference between laboring hard over an obligatory thank-you note my mother made me write after Christmas, and simply pouring my heart out to a friend over coffee at Starbucks. One was manufactured under duress. The other was the overflow of my heart.

The revelation overwhelmed me. I stood in the small classroom, worshipping, fully engaged with a very-present God. I looked up toward the ceiling and sensed that God had just poured a new understanding of prayer all over me. It was not a physical sensation, but it was just as real; golden honey of freedom, intimacy and communication poured from a pitcher in Heaven. Instinctively, I reached up to grasp the flowing stream (metaphorically) praying, "Yes, Lord, I want to talk with You this way." The Lord probably laughed—I had worked so hard at something that just needed to spill out of my heart and my mouth. How much He had to undo to get me there!

Relationship, Not Principle

I had to realize a new concept: that our attitude toward the Father in prayer is one of relationship, not primarily principle. Relationship implies that He wants the natural flow of our hearts, the overflow of conversation and companionship in our thoughts toward Him. Yes, we need to be mindful of the principles in Scripture, and yes, Scripture does dictate our behavior, but primarily we talk with our Father the way He spoke with Adam and Eve in the Garden before the Fall and the way Jesus and the disciples lived—as if we and He are walking and talking together in human form. Even in profound times of crying out to God for His help, our primary job is not to remind either God or ourselves of the truths we know; rather, it is to build a relationship of intimate sharing. In the conversation of prayer, He shares His heart with us and we share our hearts with Him.

The Process

About two years later, after my prayer life had become a natural flow of uninhibited chatter with the Lord (which, thankfully, He can endure much more easily than we humans can), I had two experiences, virtually identical, which cemented this new understanding of prayer in my heart.

The first happened during a fairly normal retreat.[4] An older woman, a friend, taught a brief segment about healing and prayer. The teaching was wonderful—it always is when she teaches—but I remember none of it. What I do remember, vividly, was the exercise she assigned after the teaching: "Go write a letter to God," she instructed. "Tell Him what you're really feeling. But then...write a letter back from Him to you."

---

[4] Shelvy Wyatt, Vineyard Women's Retreat, Vineyard New Haven, April 1991. Unpublished notes.

WHAT? I'm allowed to *do* that? How do I know that what I hear is actually God? Couldn't it be another (evil) voice? Or my own imagination? Or my own evil thoughts, or at least my misguided ones? God doesn't speak that way, does He? Isn't that just my voice I'll hear? Isn't it *dangerous*? My mind went on a road trip of anxiety and the tirade that erupted inside wouldn't stop. Perplexed, I wanted to protest. But I was far too compliant for that. And after all, I'd been on prayer teams for ages. What if someone saw me objecting? I had to go along with this, even if I didn't think it was safe.

If I was honest with myself, I was actually more concerned that I didn't think this listening would work. But I fell prey to the usual theological smokescreen. I objected on the much-more-sophisticated-basis of theology. After all, I had to be sure I wasn't being deceived. Or was that really my reason? I thought it was, but… Let's look at the real motives behind my fearful thoughts and unspoken objections.

I really trusted myself to fall into deception more than I trusted God to keep me safe. Does that make sense? I believed that something bad would probably happen and I wanted to control my environment to keep myself secure. What a negative, fearful mindset! The Scripture is very clear that if we ask for bread, the Lord will not give us a stone. And since we know that it is the Father's will that all of His children hear his voice and follow, He clearly wants to speak and to show us how to listen.

> For everyone who asks receives; he who seeks finds; and to him who knocks, the door will be opened. Which of you, if his son asks for bread, will give him a stone? Or if he asks for a fish, will give him a snake? If you, then, though you are evil, know how to give good gifts to your children, how much more will your Father in heaven give good gifts to those who ask him!" (Matthew 7:8-11)

And so, with fear and trepidation, I did as I was told. I wrote my letter to God and turned the page over. Just to be safe, I prayed that the voice I heard would be the Lord's, that the voice of the enemy would be silenced, and that my thoughts would not be distracted. "Come, Holy Spirit," I prayed, "and show me how to do this." It wasn't quite the famous "O God, help!" prayer, but it was close, and, I learned later, it's actually the perfect prayer for the situation.

On the back of my letter to God, with a new fresh page in front of me, I started to write. I wrote the words I thought God was saying. They sounded suspiciously nice. Gentle. Exhortive when necessary, but loving, caring, comforting and protecting. And soon, I was crying. It was so…reassuring. I felt loved again, cherished, and held. "I will care for you," the Lord said on my page. "Is my arm too short to heal? Have I forsaken you in the past? I have mercy on you. I will draw near to you and hold you." I could feel myself begin to relax. "For I am the strength of your heart and your portion forever," (from Psalm 73:26).

Others around me had similar experiences. Some heard and wrote just a phrase or two, but it was the right phrase for the moment, an answer from Jesus for a deep question, a solution to a troublesome dilemma. Some people even heard just one word. The right word, it seemed. Many others heard Scriptures. Others heard worship songs—ones with precisely the words they needed to hear. (Later I found that the Lord would often speak to me most clearly in worship songs.) Everyone heard God differently, but we all heard from God that day.

The key was this: we prayed and asked the Holy Spirit to speak to us, in Jesus' name. And He did. He usually does! I would like to go so far as to say He always does, but there are times when He seems dreadfully silent. Thankfully, those times are not forever and they usually occur when He is developing something much deeper in us. By and large, especially in our devotional lives, the Lord longs and yearns to speak to us as His Beloved, drawing us into deeper relationship with Him.

I was relieved that I could actually "hear" from God. I was still puzzled and concerned about my ability to get it wrong, but I decided to practice, to write more and more letters in my journal. I found, time after time, that a Scripture, a song, a word, or a God-inspired thought would bring the comfort and reassurance I needed. "I have for you life and joy. I hear your cries and I am bringing peace to your troubled heart," I would hear. "I am the shepherd and you are my sheep; You know my voice, and you follow." (from John 10:4; John 10:27)

My hearing from God wasn't consistent and I still struggled with doubts, but the Lord pursued me again and again, reminding me to listen...and to journal. A few months later, another retreat speaker, a well-respected college-ministry pastor and staffer who specialized in training prayer teams, started a morning retreat session with a similar exercise: time alone, listening to Jesus and writing down his response.[5] My mind raced back to the letter from God. There it was again, nudging me once again to more connection with the Lord. What a refreshing blessing it was to sit in the lodge that morning, pouring out my heart to the Lord, hearing His reassuring words in response.

From then on, it became a well-loved tool. When in doubt, I could always journal and He would be there. It became, and still is, the tool I fall back on the most. I am not disciplined enough to journal my letters to and from God on a daily basis. There are often long gaps in between. But it is the most trusted method I know for pulling me back into the arms of my Father.

"Write a Letter to God," along with other exercises in journaling and dialogue with God, are included in the appendix. Take a few moments to try one and see what God says.

---

[5] Doug Gregg. InterVarsity Christian Fellowship retreat, Connecticut, September, 1991. unpublished notes.

Chapter Seven
Doing What the Father is Doing: He Tells Us Specifics

Some people just "get it".

I am not one of them.

Even after learning to hear God in journaling, I still can't just "hear" *ex nihilo*[6], especially when I'm supposed to hear or when I am praying for someone. I want to hear well so I can pray accurately, but I freeze under pressure.

It seems so easy for other people. They listen for "what God is saying" and they see pictures, or feel feelings, or know information, or sense impressions, or dream dreams, or have whole visions – in technicolor, with ongoing chapters, no less.

Meanwhile, if someone says "Let's listen for what the Lord is saying," I just sit there. Nothing. Nada. Zilch. No pictures, no words, no senses (except feeling antsy, or fidgety, or wanting to get up and walk, or get something to eat). And this is *after* learning not to shut down every conceivable intuitive sense I've ever had.

But give me just one tidbit, one iota of information about what the person I'm praying for really needs, one hint at what someone else senses God is doing and I'm usually off and running. That's why I always advocate praying in a team. For

---

[6] In this case, I use *ex nihilo* not as a philosophical term, but to mean "out of context," with no relation to any previous discussion or content.

me, "team" usually means praying alongside my husband. We know each other's ways of hearing God.

I invariably start prayer ministry times by silently begging God to tell us something, anything, to set the prayer parameters. I wait, hoping that this time I will hear something obvious, tangible, and something that sounds very "God-like." Usually, nothing happens, or so I think. It's then that I lapse into the famous seven-word prayer: "Oh God, oh God, oh God, HELP!" Not a bad start, actually, but only if one exudes a tremendous amount of calm confidence on the outside while screaming to God on the inside. Fortunately, Phil recognizes my panic and generally senses something quickly, often a word, picture or Scripture (much to my relief), and I soon find myself modifying, explaining, or adding onto what he's seen. Often, the very thing he has seen so clearly has actually flown through my brain during my harangue at God.

Words of knowledge and wisdom

My church friends call the small tidbits and hints of information from God "words of knowledge" or "words of wisdom." These words give us direction and tell us what God is up to.

Technically, the two are different. A word of knowledge is knowing a fact, a bit of information, that you would not otherwise know. A word of wisdom refers more to what to do, a direction, a root cause, or a sense of how to move forward. It may be an intuition of how to apply a particular word of knowledge. Any believer can get either one at any time. Although trends do exist (my husband tends to hear more words of wisdom than words of knowledge, for example), God seems to give whatever gift seems to be necessary at the time it is needed.

In actual prayer situations, it's often difficult to tell the two apart and I maintain that it's rather unnecessary. The point is to have a clue from the Father about what He is doing. That knowledge may take many different forms.

Jesus, operating by the Holy Spirit, received revelation this way. He knew whom to pray for and He knew more about those he prayed for than they told him. He knew the thoughts of the Pharisees. He knew that the woman at the well had five husbands and was living with yet another man to whom she was not married. He knew that Peter would deny Him three times before the cock crowed. We are on safe territory as we pursue these ways of hearing from God. But that does not mean we are in *comfortable* territory. The "how" to hearing from God can take us in many interesting directions.

How we hear: Scriptural and real-life examples

A quick glance at Scripture provides amazing examples of God's varied interaction with His people.

> **Appearance and/or Audible voice:** In Genesis, Abram was ninety-nine years old when the Lord appeared to him and said, "I am God Almighty; walk before me and be blameless." (Genesis 17:1)
>
> **God speaks in the night and gives visions:** "The boy Samuel ministered before the Lord under Eli. In those days the word of the Lord was rare; there were not many visions. One night Eli, whose eyes were becoming so weak that he could barely see, was lying down in his usual place. The lamp of god had not yet gone out, and Samuel was lying down in the temple of the Lord, where the ark of God was. Then the Lord called Samuel. Samuel answered, 'Here I am.'" (1 Samuel 3:1ff)
>
> **His Word:** The Lord continued to appear at Shiloh, and there he revealed himself to Samuel through His Word. (1 Samuel 3:21)

Other people: God spoke to David through Naaman the prophet.

Dreams: "Having been warned in a dream, he [Joseph, adopted father of Jesus] withdrew to the district of Galilee, and he went and lived in a town called Nazareth." (Matthew 2:22)

Angels: "Now an angel of the Lord said to Philip, 'Go south to the road—the desert road—that goes down from Jerusalem to Gaza.'" (Acts 8:26)

Visions and audible voice: "About noon the following day as they were on their journey and approaching the city, Peter went up on the roof to pray. He became hungry and wanted something to eat, and while the meal was being prepared, he fell into a trance. He saw heaven opened and something like a large sheet being let down to earth by its four corners. It contained all kinds of four-footed animals, as well as reptiles of the earth and birds of the air. Then a voice told him, 'Get up, Peter. Kill and eat.'" (Acts 10:9-13)

Visions and angels: "At Caesarea there was a man named Cornelius, a centurion in what was known as the Italian Regiment. He and all his family were devout and God-fearing; he gave generously to those in need and prayed to God regularly. One day at about three in the afternoon he had a vision. He distinctly saw an angel of God, who came to him and said, 'Cornelius!' Cornelius stared at him in fear. 'What is it, Lord?' he asked." (Acts 10:3-4)

In addition to the scriptural argument (which we have barely begun to cover), a general look at common experience in the Church and orthodox historic tradition reveals an incredible breadth in the way the Lord communicates with us. Here is a short list of the ones I've experienced, seen or heard about:

- **Visual impression**—see a picture, or a "movie," or a part of the body that needs to be healed, or a symbol that represents something to me or the person receiving prayer
- **Mental impression**—a God-thought vs. my own thought
- **Mental insight / revelation**—a sense of direction or interpretation of events
- **Unnatural pain or sensation**—not a pain I normally have, and it is only there until reported, or until after prayer for the person suffering from such a pain
- **Scripture verse that comes to mind**
- **Song, quote or phrase**—from a conversation that "coincidentally" comes to mind
- **Emotional feeling that isn't mine**
- **Natural sign or phenomena** that can be interpreted as message
- **A vision**—a dream while awake, with a plot or motion, perhaps dialogue, and a point
- **Dream**—a dream while sleeping that is not a "normal" dream but seems to have spiritual significance
- **See a word**—a word or a series of words over someone, like a theatre marquee, a scrolling word or phrase, or a label
- **A prophecy**—a sense of what the Lord is saying, or a direct quotation from God
- **Knowing**—a sense of faith that something will occur if I pray; or a sudden surety about something; or a sense of "ought-ness;" or that God is in control of the outcome
- **Peace**—a sudden sense of peace about a situation or a potential direction
- **Tongues and/or interpretation**—a message of tongues interpreted as either prophesy or prayer
- **Overwhelming sense of compassion**—an unusual surge of compassion and desire to pray
- **An unusual urge**—an urge to do something, or to go somewhere; which might be an actual direction (from

the Lord), or descriptive of a condition, or might mean something to the person receiving prayer
- **Noticing something in the natural**—and realizing it is significant
- **Audible voice**

That's an amazing list! Whole volumes could be written on some of those. It sounds as if any thought—any random picture, Scripture verse, incident or realization could be God. In fact, the longer I listen and pray and the more I experience the ways God "speaks," the more I realize that God's voice to or through me sounds unnervingly like mine.

Having said that, I fear that many orthodox and evangelical theologians will leap to the task of explaining how heretical the very concept is. After all, I am not in any way the "I AM" of Scripture! How dare I say that God's voice sounds like mine!

His voice? My voice?

It makes sense, actually. God generally impresses His thoughts upon us in a very natural way. They come through the very abilities He has made us with—our intuitive capacities. Unfortunately, this means that every experience I have had of knowing God's voice, His way, and His direction has come through my mind, which means that "I" think it and it sounds rather like "my" voice.

On a practical level, it's easy to become immobilized trying to figure out how this works. Essentially, communication from God via the Holy Spirit is heard through sanctified right-brain intuition and instinct. It can be a gut feeling or a deep sense of knowing. But because it's intuitive, it's easy to "shut it down" by trying too hard. It's more a matter of learning what to listen *for*.

Often, listening to God means focusing on the Lord and then becoming aware of everything we hear and sense—pictures, flashes of insight, something that just "flies by" in our mind's eye. We take a chance and pay attention to that small passing glimpse and it is magnified and becomes...insight from God.

Fortunately, there is also a discernable difference between my thoughts and God's thoughts, if only slight. Perhaps it's a "tone of voice," an attitude, a turn of phrase or even content: would "I" think that thought? Have I *ever* thought that thought before? My task is therefore to learn what that "voice of God" sounds like as compared to my own voice. "It ain't easy," as the saying goes, but it is definitely possible.

A pastor once told me that learning the sound of God's voice was akin to talking on the phone with someone. The first time a person calls and does not identify himself, you may be left wondering frantically, "Who is this? Do I know this voice?" Later, however, you can identify his voice with ease.

I can distinctly remember just such a phone call. After answering and not recognizing the voice, I quickly went through an entire mental rolodex of names, trying to determine if I knew this caller who had just begun a strange conversation without identifying himself. I tried every trick I knew, asked several dozen questions and eventually determined who it must be. I launched into a long conversation, comforted by knowing who it was, only to discover, to my horror, that it was someone completely different.

But just as my pastor had assured me, once I learned my new friend's voice I could identify him instantly. It didn't take long. Hearing from God is like that. Eventually, my pastor said, I would know the tone and quality of God's voice and what it sounded like. This "God voice-print," like a fingerprint, has distinctiveness.

By faith

It would be so much nicer if these ways of hearing were easy and straightforward. Unfortunately, God does not proceed that way. He wants us to develop our faith muscle, about which I argue with Him constantly. That has not changed in 39 years of knowing Him.

Words and intuitions from Him are most often only confirmed after I speak them out. After all, these are spiritual gifts and spiritual gifts are always exercised by faith. As John Wimber noted wryly, "Faith is spelled R-I-S-K."[7] *That means you and I won't know if what we hear is from the Lord until we speak it out.* There's a risk that we haven't heard correctly or fully. I don't like that, but God doesn't seem to mind putting us into uncomfortable situations to grow and challenge us.

Often, we are tempted to think that it would have been easier operating in these gifts in Jesus' time. Then, we think, it would have been easier to hear God's voice; after all, Jesus was right there in human form. But hearing and seeing God required faith, even then. When Father spoke to Jesus from heaven, some heard the voice and said it thundered, while others claimed it was an angel speaking. (John 12:28-29) Then, as now, hearing from God is done by faith, from beginning to end.

Learning the sound of God's voice

So what does "hearing from God" actually feel like? What happens? How do I know it is God speaking? How do I learn to recognize His voice?

The most common way to start hearing is to pray in a group, often an intercessory group, and pray in the general direction that the group seems to be praying. Listen during the silences

---

[7] John Wimber, Signs and Wonders Conference Notes, 1986-7.

and notice the direction of your thoughts. And often—amazingly often—someone will pray exactly what you've been thinking. The first time it happens you may be tempted to think it's a coincidence. The second and third times, you take note. By the fourth or fifth time, you realize that you must be hearing from God. Bingo. You are.

The next step is paying attention to the circumstances of life. How many times have you "just thought about someone" when the phone rang and it was that person on the line? How often have you "happened to think of something" on the way out the door only to find that it was precisely what you needed to know for the meeting you were going to? How many times have you "suddenly realized" that something was wrong with your child so that you were able to avert a crisis? And how many times have you ignored that intuitive voice, only to realize later that it was right? You are probably already hearing from God a great deal more than you think.

Finally, it is important to act on the impressions you sense or hear. Saying them out loud, after asking God if they are appropriate for here and now and listening for His answer or urging, is a way of confirming the impressions. If they are really accurate, file them in the "that was God's voice" category. If not, file them in the "that wasn't it" file. Soon, the "got it right!" category will grow.

After a while, when you think you have the listening and hearing process well in hand, God may challenge you further. Suddenly, His voice may grow quieter or the urgings grow subtler. It's at that point that you must again take a risk and plunge ahead with faith, acting on the little you sense. His voice is still real and you have already learned to hear. If you forge ahead with care, the rewards can be enormous.

Acting on the improbable

Years ago, Phil and I were participating in a small, regional healing conference. It was during the early days of the Vineyard movement, when healing and prophetic ministry had just begun to burst on the scene of the mainline protestant, Catholic and evangelical churches. We were excited and just beginning to explore the concept of "doing what the Father is doing," but we were still very apprehensive about our ability to hear from God.

Seated awkwardly in the front row, we were officially on the prayer team for the conference, responsible to pray for anyone who wanted healing. After teaching, the pastor in charge instructed us all to listen for what the Lord wanted to do. Obedient learners that we were, we listened. I tried hard, but inwardly I was fighting with the Lord: "You know I won't hear anything Lord, so why am I even trying? Besides, if I DO hear anything, then I know I'll have to pray for someone and You won't do anything then either. So can I just leave now?" I was looking for the door. Maybe I could leave while no one was looking. I was definitely not filled with faith.

Phil, however, suddenly raised his hand. I was stunned. He'd *heard* something? "Oh no," I thought. "Now we'll have to pray." The door was looking more and more attractive.

"I have a pain in my right wrist," he said, a bit too loudly, when the pastor looked at him. Phil turned to me apologetically, "I didn't have that pain when I walked in. All of a sudden my wrist hurt. I knew it wasn't my pain," he whispered. He knew I was panicked. We'd always been in this "I can't hear from God" place together.

"Okay," the pastor said. "Anyone have a problem with their right wrist?" The room was silent. "Whew," I sighed, finally breathing again. Suddenly, a surprised "I do!" came from directly behind us. I looked around to see a man I'd never met holding his right wrist in the air. "I have my right wrist in a brace. It's an injury from an accident years ago," he explained. "I'm on vacation here and just stopped in to see what was going on." "All right," the pastor responded. "Phil, since you heard it, why don't you and...all of you (pointing in our general direction) pray for him." I tried to head for the door but I couldn't move. I was completely terrified. Clearly, Phil and I and another couple were the designated pray-ers. Wonderful. Maybe I could just die now?

We gathered to pray and asked the Holy Spirit to come and show us how to pray. We spoke to every conceivable condition, including speaking healing to the damaged wrist. I was still eyeing the door. Suddenly (it's always suddenly. God seems to like that), the gentleman we were praying for looked up. "Phil, take my wrist," he said confidently. Horrified, I watched him pull off the wrist brace and tell Phil to pull on his arm. His injured right arm. "NO," I started to yell, "don't do that!" but the man interrupted my exclamation. His eyes started tearing and he could barely talk. "You don't understand," he interjected, "I couldn't do this when I walked in." He pulled hard against Phil's tight grip. Then he moved his wrist, picked up a pen, gripped it, and tried to write. "I COULDN'T DO ANY OF THIS!" He insisted. Now he was crying.

I was prepared for failure but I was completely unprepared for success. Now what should we do? Scream? Holler? Jump up and down and let the pastor know? Be quiet? Pretend it never happened? Keep praying? (Pray for WHAT? He was HEALED!) I was looking around at the team, trying to figure out what should happen next.

But the man with the healed wrist wasn't finished. He had taken his brace completely off and was rubbing his wrist. He hadn't stopped crying. "It's healed. It's fine. But...what I really need prayer for...is my family. I'm having trouble in my family," he sobbed. "God cared enough to heal my wrist... would you pray for my family?" We were all crying by this time. But our faith level was astronomical. "Wow, He did it! God can do ANYTHING!" we thought. We dove fervently into prayer again, realizing that God had used healing to inspire faith in this visitor and now we had a huge opportunity to impact his family, his marriage, his ministry (somehow we presumed he had one), and his life. We listened again, prayed everything we heard from God, spoke healing, comfort and life to his broken heart in Jesus' name, and finally finished with several rounds of Kleenex.

Our lives had just changed and we all knew that we were completely, inevitably, and irrevocably "hooked." This God of ours had apparently leapt out of the cage we thought we had Him in and He was leading us on a hunt of a completely different kind.

Physical manifestations were only the first kind of manifestation we experienced as we waited and watched for signs of God moving and speaking. Pictures, senses, hunches, and fleeting thoughts all took on new meaning as we asked God to help us listen clearly to what He was trying to do. A bit like Aslan, the lion in Lewis' *Chronicles of Narnia*, God showed up at interesting times, and in unexpected ways.

People in small groups began to "see" pictures and visions for the first time, pictures that were accurate, detailed and life-changing. On a few occasions, words of knowledge led to evangelism and unbelievers became believers overnight. Christians whose faith had been dry and who were hopeless encountered a very real and personal Jesus who cared about the smallest of details in their lives.

There are seasons of hearing and seasons of seeing unbelievable results. And seasons of seeing… nothing. But almost always, as we launch out to act on what we sense, God "shows up" and ministers in wonderful ways, even if we don't know the results until later.

Just a few months ago, Phil saw a new face at church, a man we'd never seen there before. Without saying anything to me, Phil quietly walked over to the man during the offering and whispered a short encouragement from the Lord to him. The man showed no obvious reaction at the time but we were amazed the next Sunday to see the same man go forward in response to an invitation to come to know Jesus.

By far the most "miraculous" events we've seen have come as a result of several words of knowledge coming through different people and working together into a marvelous answer to prayer. The Lord loves to minister through His whole body and when He needs us to change direction He can let many people know in amazing ways.

A few years ago, after almost ten years in another state, the Lord made it clear through urgings, impressions, and circumstances that we should move back to the area where I grew up. We decided rather quickly and were blessed to be able to move into a new home in New England while our beautiful townhouse in a small Pennsylvania borough was still for sale. We were still living in both places for a while and many people in our old town didn't realize we had moved.

We had returned to Pennsylvania for a teaching engagement that week. At the end of our financial and emotional rope, we were tired, drained, and hopeless. We had to leave for Phil's business conference and we didn't know what to do. We both slept fitfully. I woke abnormally early that morning, tossing and turning. We hadn't heard from our realtor in weeks and our beautiful house hadn't been shown more than once in five months. Our finances had dwindled and we couldn't afford to carry the costs of two houses any longer. We were in danger of defaulting on one. Still sleepy, I retreated to the sunroom where I could fret at God without waking Phil. Actually, fretting wasn't quite the word. I ranted. "We can't do this any longer," I sobbed. (No answer). God seemed very far away. "Please do something now! This just has to turn around!" I cried and screamed at the Lord for another hour, convinced that we were about to descend into financial ruin. Had we not heard from God? I fell back asleep, dreamed badly, woke late, and ran out to an appointment. While I was gone, Phil packed up our belongings and got ready to leave.

Unbeknownst to us, a few days earlier one of our acquaintances and ministry partners was running by our house on his normal morning jog. Larry was in the habit of praying for the owners of the houses on his route, but he was surprised when he heard the words "abundant provision, more than you can ask or imagine…" as he ran by our home. He had no idea that the house was on the market, so he presumed that the message was a nudge from God to pray for us. "All right, Lord. I pray for Phil and Wendy to have abundant provision, more than they could ask or imagine," Larry prayed as he jogged.

Meanwhile, his wife, Ginny, was at home helping his parents look for a house in town. They wanted to be near their grandchildren and periodically scanned the newspapers and real estate flyers for interesting homes.

As Larry's mom looked absently at flyers, Ginny suddenly saw a "ticker tape" roll across her mind with the names "Phil and Wendy Coy" repeated over and over. She assumed it was a reminder to pray for us, so she did. At about the same time, her mother-in-law spotted our house in a real estate flyer. "What about this house?" she said, pointing to an ad that she'd scribbled over with a different phone number. "Should we look at this one?" The picture was barely visible underneath the thick marker lines of phone numbers, but Ginny peered closely. "I think that's Phil and Wendy's house!" she exclaimed. "But it can't be! It's not for sale! I've always wanted that house, but I knew I could never afford it and I wanted to be content with what I had. It can't be that house, can it?" She almost ignored the ad, thinking that it was a mistake. Then she remembered the ticker-tape message and decided to call the realtor. Yes, she discovered, it *was* our house and it was for sale.

Larry, Ginny, and Larry's parents knew they had to pray, but this time their family prayer meeting led to some surprising results. Within a few days, the Lord completely changed the course of their lives by confirming with Scriptures, visions, words, pictures and circumstances that Larry, Ginny, and Larry's parents should move into our house. To their amazement, the house was affordable and available. The abundant provision, more than they could ask or imagine, was actually for them.

Meanwhile, Phil and I were late and getting later. My whole morning had been delayed because I overslept, and every appointment went longer than usual. Phil was not amused when I walked in the door. As we were just about to descend into an all-out war, the phone rang. "Are you sitting down? This is your realtor-angel," our realtor joked. In no mood for humor, Phil grunted, "Yeah, okay. What is it? We're about to walk out the door." Then he really did sit down. To our amazement, we had a full-price offer on the very day I had screamed out to God. "My timing is always perfect," he heard the Lord whisper as we got into the car.

For years, we didn't share these bits and pieces, random fragments of thoughts or images, thinking they were "just us," "weird," or worse yet, "distractions." But what would have happened if Ginny hadn't paid attention to the ticker tape message and missed the opportunity for her dream house? What would have happened if Phil had ignored the pain in his wrist and didn't speak up?

Words of knowledge often look and sound more like puzzle pieces than specific instructions. They are routinely incomplete, confusing, and odd-sounding. But they mesh to create an opportunity for God to break in, often in miraculous ways.

How often we pray in a group, listening for what the Lord wants to do, when many different and seemingly isolated words converge to give us direction. One person hears the word "unity." Another sees a picture of two people coming together; yet another sees two parts of a broken heart becoming one; and another hears a Scripture about reconciliation. Suddenly we are praying for the healing of a broken marriage.

As we learn to listen, it's amazing how often those words come together to form incredible treasure maps for our lives and the lives of those around us.

Chapter Eight
Getting Practical:
An Exercise in Listening Prayer

Over the last 25 years, Phil and I have been to hundreds of churches and conferences, prayed for thousands of people, and watched thousands more get prayer from other team members. By far the most potent prayer times have been when we heard direction from the Lord and prayed those things. In those spaces and times when we are watching and listening, silence is always unnerving. What do I do if the Lord doesn't say anything? What if He doesn't "show up?" But as we listen to God and equip others to do so, He always does "show up." He reveals what He is doing because He loves to encourage His people; and it is always amazing.

Because most of us are insecure in our ability to hear from God and to minister effectively in prayer, we often resort to asking questions and gathering information so that we know better how to pray. It's necessary to have background and history if we are to pray effectively and accurately, especially in "inner healing" situations, but we need to grow in our confidence and ability to hear from God, even when we receive little corroborating information.

We don't always have the luxury of long conversations with those we are about to pray for. For example, I might not have time to have a long discussion with a person who comes forward for prayer in a large conference setting or after a sermon. The music may be too loud, there may be long lines of people watching and waiting, or the setting may be too public.

Similarly, if God nudges me, (or I have an inclination) to pray for a clerk in the checkout line at the supermarket, I probably shouldn't ask a lot of questions before praying for her broken heart or her injured wrist. In fact, delaying the line may have the opposite effect from what I want: I might inspire the wrath of the clerk *and* her customers, not because I said the name of Jesus but because I held up the line. What do I do when I have absolutely no information at all about a person?

We've led a listening prayer exercise for almost 20 years. It was taught to us by a prayer ministry specialist and trainer who used it for years before that. We've never seen it fail in any gathering we've led. You might think that's because we're amazing leaders, but we're not—it's not about us. Instead, it works because God wants to communicate His love to us, through Jesus Christ and by the Holy Spirit, much more than we can imagine. He is just waiting to intervene and to teach us new ways to hear from him and to pray for others. He wants to meet our need and desires nothing more than intimate relationship and communion (dialogue and intimacy) with each of us.

But it all starts with that risky faith, hearing from Him and acting on what we hear.

Why don't you try this exercise? The ideal number of people for this activity is four but you can try it with three. It doesn't work as well with two (too few people to listen and pray—and therefore too much pressure on the pray-ers) or more than four (it takes too much time for five or more people). It also helps if you don't know each other well since it's harder to determine if you're hearing from God when you know the people well.

Once you have seen how it works, this exercise is simple. The goal is to practice listening to God and praying for each other. Leadership rotates around the group so that everyone has the chance to participate. Being the leader isn't scary—it just involves opening and closing the prayer time. Everyone has a chance to listen; everyone has a chance to share what they've sensed, seen, or heard; and everyone has a chance to receive prayer.

Here is how the exercise works[8]:

1) Find a watch with a second hand, or a stopwatch. (You need to be able to tell at a glance when two or three minutes have gone by).

2) Introduce yourselves to each other (but don't give any personal information. Name and where you're from is plenty).

3) Sit close enough in a circle so you can see one another and easily reach one another (in case you want to lay hands on a person when you pray for him or her, or if you want to hold hands in a circle).

4) Designate one person to be the leader. (It's helpful if this person has at least some experience listening to God but it's not essential. This role will rotate around the circle).

5) The person to the leader's left will receive prayer first. This role will also move around the circle. As you receive prayer, keep your eyes closed and focus on the Lord. It's most helpful to the people praying if you do not look up and stare at them while they're trying to listen or pray.

---

[8] If you have a number of groups participating, it's better to have someone oversee the whole room. That person can be the timekeeper for all the groups instead of having someone in each group do it. Also, the person overseeing the whole room can direct the entire exercise, telling the Leader and the groups what steps to do and when. This facilitates prayer and allows a whole roomful of groups to do the same thing at once. It's best to be very directive from the front so that the groups don't devolve into chaos: "All right, now listen...." "Now pray what you've heard...." "Now check in with the person you're praying for".... Etc.

6) Appoint another person to act as the timekeeper, neither the leader nor the person receiving prayer. This role will also rotate.

7) Before you begin the exercise, have someone pray that the time will be effective: Ask the Lord to show you what He is doing, to release vision and words of knowledge and anything He wants to show the group. Ask Him to teach you how to listen and pray. And authoritatively shut down any voice of the enemy or any distraction, since it's the Lord's voice you want to hear.

8) Leader: If it's comfortable for you and the group, ask the person you are praying for if you (all) may lay hands on him or her. If you are allowed to lay hands on that person and are comfortable then do so. If not, that's fine! Alternately, you can simply pray separately or hold hands in the circle. Whatever you feel comfortable with is fine.

9) Leader: Ask the Holy Spirit to come and show you how to pray. He is the one who gives insight, revelation, wisdom, and words of knowledge; and He always leads us to Jesus. This prayer should only take 30 seconds, maximum.

10) Now everyone listen—in complete quiet—for two minutes. It will seem like an eternity. The timekeeper can keep track and let the group know when two minutes is up. Notice anything that comes to mind that seems to be from the Lord: pictures, senses, feelings, impressions, words, Scriptures; anything that might be an inkling from the Lord.

11) For about the next two minutes (timekeeper take note), everyone except the person receiving prayer may pray or say anything he or she has heard or sensed or seen. If you can, pray it specifically for the person receiving

prayer. Otherwise, just describe what you heard or saw. For example: "I see a waterfall and I think it means that the Lord wants to refresh you with living water. So I minister the refreshment of the Lord all over you, in Jesus' name, running down and washing your mind, your heart, your hands…The cleansing and refreshing of the Lord. Come, Lord, and refresh!" Etc. [Note to the person receiving prayer: stay in an attitude of prayer and accept what is given as a gift from the Lord, if it seems true to what God is doing in your life.] Finish when all have had a chance to pray what they've heard or sensed, or in two minutes. Don't let it go on too long or you may be praying for hours! This exercise needs to stay short. Note: if you do not hear anything or sense anything that the Lord is doing, you may always bless the person, or pray to affirm what God is already doing in his or her life. He or she will feel loved and that's always good! For example, "I bless you, Sarah, as a daughter of the King. I bless you with His pleasure and His comfort, His care in the midst of all you're going through," etc. It doesn't take a word of knowledge to bless someone with the pleasure of the Lord.

12) Next, take two or three minutes for everyone to check in with the person you're praying for. Did any of what you prayed or said make any sense? Did it "ring true?" Did it mean anything to him or her? If not, that's okay! (Maybe it was the pizza you had for lunch.) Don't be offended. Since you are all just trying this, you may or may not hear something that is pertinent. Now ask what the person REALLY needs prayer for—in brief. Find out just a little about what he or she would like God to do. Remember, you only have two to three minutes (Timekeeper, take note).

13) For the next two or three minutes, everyone can pray again for the pray-ee, this time with knowledge. Pray for

God to accomplish all that you heard that seemed to be accurate and helpful. AND pray for any requests the person shared. Knowing that person's needs should make it much easier.

14) Leader: At the end of those few minutes of prayer, finish by sealing what God has done in Jesus' name or by asking the Holy Spirit to do so; Ask God to continue His work and end in Jesus' name.

15) That's it! Now the roles of leader, pray-ee, and timekeeper all rotate one person to the LEFT. The new leader is the person you just prayed for. The new pray-ee is the person to the new leader's left. The new timekeeper is someone who hasn't done it before. As before, the new leader asks permission and starts the prayer time, and ends prayer when the whole cycle is finished.

Lather, rinse, repeat. Do the whole process two or three more times until you are back to the beginning person again and everyone has had a chance to receive prayer.

If you need a reminder, refer to the one-page summary of the exercise in the appendix.

Whew! You made it! That's the hardest it will ever be.

Think about and discuss the experience within your circle or in the group at large. Did people have something prayed over/for them that could only have been from God? Was this the first time that you felt you heard from God? Was this a comfortable exercise? What was surprising to you?

Chapter Nine

Doing What the Father is Doing: Watching

The basement classroom was filled with teens eyeing each other for possible dates. At least, we hoped it was just dates they were contemplating. We started our weekly youth group meeting as usual. The youth leader prayed for the Spirit's presence and we began to sing, worship, and focus on Jesus. Exuberant praise led to quiet intimacy. I had my hands up and my eyes closed but I stopped my idyllic reverie with the Lord long enough to peek at the young crowd around me.

Several girls were clutching Kleenexes and looking a bit flushed. A few boys on the other side were blinking quickly and looking at the floor, sniffling. It wasn't flu season. This had to be the work of the Holy Spirit. One of the younger girls suddenly jumped up and ran out of the room and an alert leader soon followed her into the hallway. Bathroom visit? Looking for drugs? Phone call? The possibilities were endless. After all, this was a group of street-wise kids. We joked that on an average night several kids came to the Lord and we called the police only once. The gang wannabes were slowly learning to encounter Jesus but they hadn't lost their street-wise ways yet. I watched the conversation in the hallway, keeping an eye on the door.

"What is it?" the leader asked. "I feel weird. I think I need to go home. I think it's the flu," the girl responded. "What do you mean?" the leader probed further. "Well, I feel, sort of... feverish. And dizzy. And my face feels hot. And I think I have this eyelid thing going on or something. And I feel like I'm going to pass out. And I'm kinda shaky. I think I have the flu or something." My friend laughed. "No, honey, it's the Holy Spirit.

Does it actually feel bad?" "No, it kinda feels good, but weird."
Undaunted, my friend persisted. "Does God feel closer, or
farther away?" "Uhhhhh..." This was clearly a new category
the teen hadn't thought of before... "Uhhh.... Closer I guess. I
never thought about that. Closer. Weird. Closer. Does He DO
that?"

"Okay, time for Holy Spirit 101," I thought. These young people
had never felt the presence of God. Of course, a good many of
them had emotional wounds so deep it would take a spiritual
backhoe to get to them; a part of the reaction around the room
was their pain surfacing. But that wasn't bad either. It was all
part of the process. Surface the pain; take it to Jesus, ask the
Holy Spirit to fill the place the pain had been... I rehearsed the
process, planning in advance what to say later.

The first issue I would need to address was our behavior as a
team. Why did we all have our eyes closed? Yes, we were
worshipping. But what about when we prayed for the kids or
responded to what was going on in the room? We were used to
praying with our eyes closed and singing with our eyes open.
The new order would be to worship with our eyes closed and
pray with our eyes open. Closed eyes = worship and intimacy
with Jesus. Open eyes = see what God is doing.

"*See* what God is doing? Can you *SEE* that?" I could imagine
what they would say. Clearly, I had my work cut out for me. A
few leaders would know what I meant. A great many more
would be clueless.

Just as I was about to get impatient in my reverie the Holy Spirit
stopped me. "Wait. Don't get judgmental, Wendy. This isn't
new territory for you, is it?" I shook my head, suddenly
remembering how far I'd come. It wasn't long ago that I'd been
asking the exact same question: How in the world could you
SEE God working?

You can't, always. But I seriously doubt that the Gentiles in Cornelius's house in Acts 10 were calm, cool, and collected when they heard Peter speak about Jesus; the Holy Spirit descended on them and they spoke in tongues.[9] They were Romans. They were having an encounter with the Holy Spirit. They were praising God. Do you think they were *quiet*?

Likewise, the apostles and believers in the upper room were filled with the Spirit. They also had a reaction, one that was physical enough for onlookers to tease them about being drunk. Sometimes, when the Holy Spirit is dramatically impacting someone it is a physical event. We need to watch so we know what to do.

Think of it this way. The Holy Spirit is large and, well, a Spirit. He is, after all, the Creator of the Universe. We, on the other hand, are small and human. When the spiritual and the human realm meet, there is a reaction. What that reaction will be is anyone's guess. Emotions are stirred and very human responses occur. Sometimes it looks strange. Sometimes it doesn't. Sometimes a person's very human tendencies and emotional brokenness predispose him or her to extreme emotional reactions. Sometimes the Spirit is healing very deep wounds, which then brings human pain and emotional response to the surface in a visible way. In short, our bodies react.

---

[9] While Peter was still speaking these words, the Holy Spirit came on all who heard the message. The circumcised believers who had come with Peter were astonished that the gift of the Holy Spirit had been poured out even on the Gentiles. For they heard them speaking in tongues and praising God. Then Peter said, "Can anyone keep these people from being baptized with water? They have received the Holy Spirit just as we have." So he ordered that they be baptized in the name of Jesus Christ. (Acts 10:44-48)

In Scripture, we see many different reactions when human beings interact with the Holy Spirit or with spiritual beings. For example, most biblical encounters with an angel involve someone being afraid. Why else would heavenly messengers customarily begin their words to men with "Do not fear?" It seems that angels are big, out of the ordinary, important, and, well, *scary*. When we encounter them, we respond.

Similarly, we sometimes respond when the Holy Spirit begins to reveal the love of Jesus to us, although those encounters shouldn't breed fear. Sometimes we are still and quiet. Sometimes we shake. Sometimes our eyelids flutter, or heat rises in our face or hands, or we feel lightheaded or even faint. Sometimes we "glow" with perspiration or a look of joy, sometimes our muscles contract as if we have been physically impacted. Sometimes we feel the Lord's presence. Sometimes we feel peace. Sometimes we want to laugh or dance. Sometimes we have no reaction at all.

There are times when the agitation in a person's physical behavior during prayer tempts onlookers to think his or her movement is demonically inspired, not Holy Spirit inspired. I'm rather cautious in those circumstances because there's nothing worse than attributing to the enemy what is really God. ("Woe to those who call evil good and good evil" Isaiah 5:20). But if discernment leads me to believe something demonic is occurring, I generally quiet down the prayer situation and close it. I can follow up later with more in-depth interview and prayer or refer the person to another prayer team. Most of the time, this is not the case, however, and we rest assured that the Holy Spirit has come with His gifts to encourage His people.

The manifestations—or signs—of the Spirit at work are as varied as what He does inside us, and we respond in just as many varied ways. As soon as we think we have seen every possible response, another one occurs. Keep in mind, it's not necessarily the Spirit causing the reaction or making us do anything in particular. It is usually *our reaction* to the Spirit's work. The reaction itself can be controlled and stopped, or allowed.[10] Most of the time the reaction is not excessive and is a clear sign that the Holy Spirit is doing something. We want to allow and encourage the work of the Spirit. We notice the response, redirect our prayers if we need to, and focus on the Lord and how He is drawing near. "Lord, what are you doing? Show us more! Do more, Lord!"

It's important to recognize that we do live in a real, concrete world. The Holy Spirit is not offended if we encourage someone to press the pause button on His activity in order to stay safe. If I'm driving when the Holy Spirit suddenly reveals something to me or makes His presence known, and I start to shake or cry, it's probably best either to compose myself or to pull over to the side of the road until I am calm enough to drive again. I've known friends who encountered the Holy Spirit and could easily have been charged with DUI if they had been behind the wheel, but they had assuredly not been drinking or drugging.

The Holy Spirit gives us much to see when He's active and there's much to learn when we pray for people. Generally, we're wise to keep our eyes open and see what God is doing. That can often inform our prayers. For example, if I pray encouraging words from the Lord over my friend and she suddenly starts nodding in affirmation and crying, I have a fairly good clue that she is responding either to my prayer or to a work of the Holy Spirit. I am inclined to watch closely, ask the Holy Spirit what He is doing, and continue praying in that general direction. If the Holy Spirit is strongly "touching" her, she may be weak-in-the-knees or feel faint. I may support her if she starts to fall to the floor, so she feels protected. Or I may help her to a seat so

---

[10] We assuredly do not want to stop what the Spirit is doing, but it is important to note that we are still "self-controlled"—our reactions are either allowed or disallowed by us. We should not blame the Holy Spirit for "making us" out of control.

that I can continue to pray for her while she is fully aware and participating. Most of the time, I'd rather the person I'm praying for be alert and engaged so he or she can actively receive and appropriate all that is prayed and all that God is doing.

In addition, the Holy Spirit may want us to notice the physical condition of the person receiving prayer.

Once, at a conference when I was new to prayer teams, I watched as a leader prayed for a young woman. The woman was intently focused on the Lord but the leader was intently focused on her. The leader asked her a few questions and she responded by naming some vague and rather generic symptoms, though she didn't stop focusing on Jesus. Then, suddenly, he spoke to her heart, telling it to be healed and strong in Jesus name. "How did you know?" she asked, incredulously.

I was astounded. What did he see or hear? I pushed into the circle closer so I could hear. So did all of the other team members. "How did you know that? Did you hear that? What did you see? What just happened?" we all chattered at the same time. "You thought that was a word of knowledge, didn't you?" He laughed as he challenged us. "You have to look. You have to keep your eyes open! It wasn't a word of knowledge, at least not most of it. I heard her symptoms. I saw her nails—they were severely bent and blue."

Apparently he knew of a medical condition which was typified by her symptoms. Her physical appearance was his first clue. "That's when I knew," he explained. "You have to WATCH, people!" Having suspected the source of the problem, he was then free to speak to the real issue—her heart. Note: This is not license to diagnose or verify medical conditions. But in this case, the prayer leader was right. He took all of the symptoms and his observations into account and prayed for wisdom. He got it and the authority to pray. We don't know if the young woman was completely healed. We do know she was impacted. That was enough to help us learn our lesson.

Watching can serve another purpose as well: it may keep us from going in the wrong direction. There are times when someone reacts negatively to what is being prayed. In those instances, I back off and ask the Holy Spirit what to do next. Often, I will stop praying out loud or quiet down and finish the prayer session. After all, this is about the person and his or her interaction with the Lord. I don't in any way want to interfere! If I am going in a direction that is not comfortable for the person I'm praying for, it will make it more difficult for him or her to receive from the Lord. So, even if it's what I think God is actually doing (or wants to do), I will pause and take my cues from the person.

That's a radical concept, actually. The focus of our prayer is Jesus... AND the people we're praying for. We listen to Him, but we minister to them. Their dignity, their comfort and their ability to receive are the primary concerns. If they can't receive what is being ministered, the prayer may even hurt the work God wants to do in the long run.

We are only the handmaidens and butlers at this wedding banquet. The bridegroom and the bride are meeting (either individually or corporately) and we do not ever want to get in the way. Our primary job is to lead people to Jesus, in whatever way is best for them, and then get out of the way. We are just facilitators of His intimate activity. It's not really what we are doing, but what *He* is doing, that matters.

Recently, I visited another church in the area on Pentecost Sunday. I sat next to a young woman who had attended one of our seminars but I did not know her well. I did know that she had a profound encounter with Jesus after our seminar, but I didn't know more than that.

As we worshipped during communion, she was trembling slightly. Smiling inside at the appropriateness of the day for such encounters (after all, it was Pentecost), I quietly reached over and laid my hand on her shoulder, praying under my breath, affirming and blessing what the Holy Spirit was doing. Her eyes were closed in worship. Her hands trembled a bit more, she was crying, her eyelids fluttered, and she lifted her face toward the Lord she was encountering. She seemed far away. Suddenly, embarrassed and perhaps confused, she remembered where she was, in a traditional church with people she didn't know, and stopped worshiping. Holding her arm tightly, she tried to stop her hand from shaking. "It's okay," I reassured her. "It's the Spirit." She nodded and we both went back to praying; I prayed for her and she met with the Lord. It was a sweet encounter that reminded me again of the importance of keeping our eyes open and watching, and the importance of making space for what the Holy Spirit is doing. How much there is to see as we pray!

I'm also amazed at how much direction we receive when we watch. Responses to our prayers give us huge clues that can make us much more effective.

Recently, a woman we know—let's call her Jessica—came to us with a prayer need. She was struggling at home, unhappy with her own reactions to her family. She wasn't sure exactly why but she knew her responses just weren't right. A friend and I prayed, asking God what He was doing. I thought I sensed a few fleeting impressions, all good, and I prayed those over Jessica. I was actually rather proud of myself. I had heard words I didn't expect, and I thought they were rather (*pause for self-aggrandizement*)... helpful.

Suddenly, my friend knelt down and took Jessica's hands. Staring at her intently, she said, "I just think the Lord wants you to know... you are *not* your mother!" Surprised, I watched. And without a sound, Jessica began to weep and then sob. I grabbed the ever-present Kleenex box, and my friend and I began again to pray. Suddenly, the direction was much clearer. We knew what to break, what to speak to, what to do. We knew what God was doing. All it took was a glance.

Lastly, we watch not only what the Father is doing visibly with the pray-ee but we communicate with our other team members as well. Phil and I pray together frequently for other people. Many times I know to give Phil the lead as we pray for someone because his look tells me that he has heard something significant. Sometimes he will nod to me because we both know that the direction of prayer is one I am more familiar with. After 25 years of praying together for all manner of illnesses, concerns, and emotional needs, we are well acquainted with each others' looks and we have a whole language available to us as we use our eyes. When Phil rolls his eyes and sighs, I know he has heard something but feels reluctant to pray it. My eyes communicate back to him silently: "Just say it!" Other times, I know it's up to me to follow up on a prayer point, which is confirmed when he gives me a pointed look. On occasion he will glance at me and I'll nod and point to another team member: "She's supposed to pray now." We're communicating with each other.

God gives us many signposts and indicators of what He is doing as we pray for people. We watch carefully and keep our eyes open so we don't miss any of them!

Chapter Ten
What Do I Do With What I Hear and See?

The most crucial step in our journey to hear from God and to do what He's doing is not the "seeing or hearing from Him" part. That's the first step and it requires faith, but the next step is really more important. It determines the effectiveness of what we pray.

Here is the crucial question: now that I've started, even tentatively, to hear from God...what do I do with what I hear? Of course this question is soon followed by others. How do I know it's Him? How does what I see fit into the overall picture? Is discernment part of the process?

There are quick and easy answers for those questions but they deserve more unpacking. The fast answers are these: What you do with what you hear depends on the circumstances and what God is doing. How do you know it's Him? Although you can't know for certain except in hindsight, you can start by checking to see if what you're hearing is scriptural. How does what you see fit into the overall picture? Try praying or saying it and see; the picture often evolves over time. Is discernment part of the process? Yes. Always.

That was the abridged "thumbnail" version, if you will. But you probably want more than that. I know I do, even after twenty-five years.

Discernment

Three questions can help with discernment:

1) **Is what you are hearing consistent with Scripture?** Even though a word of knowledge is revelation it is never a new revelation that goes beyond Scripture and the revelation of Jesus. God will not contradict His Word. For example, He will not tell someone to commit adultery, no matter how "right" the relationship feels. However, although alignment with Scripture is a primary consideration, most of the time it does not apply.

A word of knowledge is often very specific to a particular situation and has nothing to do with Scripture at all. A picture of a certain model of car, a word giving direction for a new job, or a warning not to be distracted by a particular task are not words which can be confirmed by Scripture. For example, when a friend prayed for me recently she saw a picture of a mill in a swiftly flowing river. She heard an exhortation not to place a mill in the river of the Holy Spirit's power. I knew the picture was a warning to concentrate more on the writing task the Lord had given me and less on my handcrafting business. The picture was not one that could be confirmed or denied with Scripture.

Other pictures are consistent with scriptural images or concepts, but the Scripture does not offer clarity about their accuracy or what to do with them. Nor can the Scripture tell us what those pictures mean. A picture of a refreshing waterfall and a word about a new open door are each consistent with Scripture and may be exactly what the person I'm praying for needs to hear. But how do I know whether those pictures or words are correct? Are they appropriate for the moment and the person's needs? These questions require another level of discernment.

2) **Is what you are hearing confirmed by someone else?** The most important response comes from the person you're praying for. He or she may immediately know if the word applies. Someone else may receive the same word or something close to it. Another person may have a sense that the word is true for a certain time and place. Keep in mind that regardless of confirmation it is possible for true words of knowledge *not* to be acknowledged, even though they are true. The person you're praying for may be embarrassed, ashamed, or unwilling to address the issue. Or the word may be for later. It may require time and intercession before it actually happens or before it is applied.

3) **Is what you are hearing confirmed by other words of knowledge?** Often a word of knowledge makes sense only when another word is given. For example, an image of snowflakes sensed by one pray-er may be further clarified when another person hears "though our sins are as scarlet, He will make us whiter than snow."

What about the meaning and application of pictures such as the refreshing waterfall or the open door? What do I do with those words? What do they mean? Do they apply now? If so, how? In order to know what to do next, I need to understand that what I see and hear from the Lord is only part of the overall picture.

Revelation, Interpretation, and Application

One of the most overlooked keys to dealing with any form of insight, whether it be prophetic words, words of knowledge, intuitions or pictures, is that a revelation has three parts: the revelation itself, the interpretation, and the application. We rarely separate them yet doing so can avoid many kinds of trouble.

Most of our mistakes in hearing from God actually do not involve the revelation itself. Instead, we usually miss the interpretation or mangle the application. Worse yet, we think it's our responsibility to do all three so we try to figure out an interpretation when we don't have one; or we attempt to apply a principle or an interpretation when all we had was a simple picture.

Revelation

The safest way to "do what the Father is doing" is simply to say or pray the revelation itself. If that's all you have then only do that! The revelation is the picture, the word, the feeling, the Scripture, or the thought. Often, one person has the revelation and another person has an interpretation or an application. One person does not need to do all three. Once again, ask God for the right piece to the puzzle at the right time. If you see a picture or word while praying, ask God what to do with it. If the urge to say it remains, then speak it out and see if anyone else has something to add.

Interpretation

The interpretation is riskier. It is, quite simply, the meaning of the revelation; we should pray specifically for that meaning. It is not always as obvious as it may seem. For example, a waterfall may indicate a time of refreshing. Or it may symbolize streams of cleansing. It might mean that rain is coming after a drought. Or, taken quite literally, it may signify that a vacation at Niagara Falls is in order.

Most importantly, the most likely person to know the interpretation of any revelation is the person for whom you are praying. If you sense that you have an interpretation of a particular word and it seems appropriate to say it, try asking the person if it makes sense. The person probably knows.

Application

The application is even more difficult to determine but a team effort makes it much easier. Most often, as with the interpretation, the person receiving the prayer is the one who will understand the application. If he or she knows how it applies…well, then, that is how it applies! That beautiful waterfall may mean the pray-ee is supposed to go to Niagara Falls instead of a long-planned vacation in Arizona. Or, it could mean that times of refreshing are just about to fall after a long season of trial. Ask the Lord, ask the person you're praying for, and wait and see. The application may unfold in time or another person may see it clearly. Remember, we are only responsible to do what the Father shows us to do.

Above all, since the responsibility for application lies with the person receiving prayer, we must be careful about "advice-giving" in this context.

We have a perfect scriptural example of this. In the book of Acts, Paul was warned by Agabus, the prophet, not to go to Jerusalem. When the people heard the prophecy, they all pleaded with him not to go. But Paul, having heard the consequences from a clear prophetic word, chose to ignore their application of the prophecy, admonished them for making it harder on him, and acted on the application that he knew was right for him—he went anyway.

> Coming over to us, he [Agabus] took Paul's belt, tied his own hands and feet with it and said, "The Holy Spirit says, 'In this way the Jews of Jerusalem will bind the owner of this belt and will hand him over to the Gentiles.'" When we heard this, we and the people there pleaded with Paul not to go up to Jerusalem. Then Paul answered, "Why are you weeping and

breaking my heart? I am ready not only to be bound, but also to die in Jerusalem for the name of the Lord Jesus." When he would not be dissuaded, we gave up and said, "The Lord's will be done." (Acts 21:11-14)

We can rest in the knowledge that the application of prophecy is not our responsibility. It is up to the person we're praying for, and the Lord.

Wisdom and Timing

Ultimately, we need wisdom in every situation. There aren't any easy answers to determine if what we hear is from God and how it applies. Once again, these spiritual gifts operate by ~~faith~~ R-I-S-K. However, the best practice is to go back to the Lord in dialogue continually asking for wisdom. Dialogue involves two-way conversation but too often we are content to hear only the first bit of the exchange. Ask more! "What do I do with this, Lord? Is it from You? Is it for now? Do I need to wait until later? How does it apply? Tell me more!"

We are most in danger when we become accustomed to hearing and therefore presume that we know how something applies. Every interchange, every personal struggle, every phone call deserves fresh wisdom. Every person needs something different, and each person may need something different than he or she did the last time we prayed.

Groups, too, need different messages at different times. The Apostle Paul was aware of this. He readily administered grace to the Galatians, but admonished the Corinthians strongly, giving them standards, exhortation, and clear direction. Both the Galatians and the Corinthians received godly answers to behavioral issues—but very different answers. What would have happened if Paul had advised the Galatians to continue to abide by the law which they had been given? How would the Corinthians have responded if Paul had merely encouraged them with even more freedom and grace, which are classic hallmarks of the Gospel?

Even in large group ministry situations when the stated direction for prayer is very specific (e.g. receiving the Father's love, or forgiving your neighbor) one person might need a prayer that is different. You may be that person! I'm often tempted to feel "left out" when my experience during large group ministry times is different than everyone else's. I need to remind myself continually that I am not missing out and the Lord is doing something distinct and specific with me. Similarly, if you are not "receiving" in the same mode as everyone else, then the Lord is probably doing something different with you. Perhaps in that moment you should be a pray-er, rather than the pray-ee. Perhaps you will have exactly the right word at the right time for one particular person. Each situation will be unique. Look for it. Expect it. We are all individuals, so Jesus has individual responses for each of us.

To some He said, "Your faith has made you well," and to others, "Go wash," and to still others, "I am willing (that is, I WANT to heal you). Be clean!" To another He said, "Go and sin no more." He raised one young man from the dead just because He cared and was moved with compassion.

One answer does not fit all similar situations. We must not generalize. A specific answer in one instance should not become a principle and a principle should not become the One True Application for every setting. Even when a scriptural principle does apply, it does not necessarily apply to every similar situation every time.

Similarly, just because God is teaching you a particular truth does not mean that it is what the person you're praying for needs to hear. It *might* be. Since you thought about it at that particular moment it may be a clear indication that God is behind it. However, to be safe you need to double-check with

God. Don't make an assumption. Otherwise, you run the risk of projecting your own answers and issues onto an unsuspecting victim, missing completely what the Lord is doing.

Let's say my friend, Rachel, has a sprained ankle. She desperately wants God to heal her so that she does not have to go to the doctor. She asks me to pray. If God has been teaching me to believe that He still heals miraculously, I may think that is what Rachel needs to hear as well. Seeing an opportunity to try my new-found principle, I launch into a faith-filled proclamation of healing, aimed generally at Rachel, but also reminding God of His promises. But what if God is actually doing something different? What if He is saying that He won't heal the ankle that way but wants to heal Rachel's fear of doctors? If I haven't listened to Him first, I might miss God's better way.

This process of hearing is always relational. We talk with the Lord and He responds. *Then* we filter what we hear through the principles of Scripture and the truth that He has already revealed. The analysis always follows the dialogue, not the other way around. We talk, listen, check the validity of what we've heard, and then *do*. That way we avoid thinking of God as if He were a Holy Box of Principles from which we can pull a truth at any time and apply it at will. If my prayers are largely consumed with reminding God of words He has already spoken in Scripture, insisting that He fulfill those promises right now, I may miss the opportunity to listen for what He is *actually* doing in the moment. He knows which piece of His Word to use, what wisdom to impart in any given situation, and which principle to avoid. Our job is just to listen.

Listen…and then ask Him about how much to say and do.

Wait. Did you catch that "how much?" Don't we just pray everything we hear? Nope. We ask what to do with it. Remember, that's the interpretation and application part.

Even the Lord did not say all of what He knew. He knew when to be quiet. For example, at some point He knew he would go to Jerusalem, be crucified, and rise again, but He did not share that knowledge until the right time. He did not tell Judas that he would betray Him until the last moment; instead He gave Judas every opportunity to repent. He did not tell Mary and Martha, when they sent word that their brother Lazarus was ill, that Lazarus would die and be raised from the dead. He did not tell the woman at the well that she had had five husbands and was living with another man until *after* she told Him that she had no husband. He did not share any more than what His Father told Him to say. He knew very well what to do and how to wait until the right time.

Even today, Jesus waits to give information. He waits so that we have time to make our own choices. He waits so that we can assimilate and respond well to what He says. He waits until the Father says it is the right time.

In any given situation, as you pray, how do you know if it is that "right time" to pray, or which direction to go? Should you pray the picture or image you see? Should you wait and intercede? Should you pray that what you see *does* happen or that it *doesn't* happen? For example, if I see a waterfall, do I pray for a waterfall of refreshing or do I pray that water does not flood the house?

Ask Jesus! He did not, and does not, give the same answers every time, even in the same situation. He alone knows what the person we're praying for can handle and what will bring life. Ask! He will tell you. His desire is to bring abundant life to overcome the kingdom of darkness with His Kingdom of Light, and He knows exactly the right words to make it happen.

Doing What the Father is Doing:
The Kingdom of God
and Authority

Chapter Eleven
The Kingdom of God and Healing: A Broader Context

While I watched and learned and prayed and copied, Phil studied. For my husband, one of the most crucial steps in any learning process is overcoming theological objections. His good evangelical and New-England-intellectual-Protestant-work-ethic upbringing kept him from all sorts of heresy and evil. Faced with new ideas about prayer that he'd never heard before, he was eager, but cautious. His quick response was, wisely, to go to prayer, Scripture, church history and a good study of theology.

He tore through our notes, our theology textbooks and our Bibles to see where to start. The first step he soon discovered was the need to understand the Kingdom of God.

In the United States, we don't have a good concept of a kingdom. Given our revolutionary birth in the late 1700's, our country is steeped in an anti-kingdom mentality. Considering the abuses our forefathers suffered from kings, that's not surprising. Fortunately, this mentality has allowed us to be a refreshingly independent and entrepreneurial country, forward-thinking and innovative.

But regrettably, we have also missed out entirely on concepts of how the Lord operates as our King and how His Kingdom functions.

Any good royal will tell you that a kingdom is where a king reigns. Jesus was well aware of the concept and He consistently preached, "The kingdom of God is near. Repent and believe the good news!" A quick search of the Gospels shows at least 50 references to the Kingdom or the Kingdom of God with another 25 or so references in the rest of the New Testament.

Kingship was not a foreign concept to Jesus' Jewish audience or to Paul's gentile one. They lived under Herod and Caesar (neither gentle nor goodly nor godly kings, but kings nevertheless).

Jesus didn't explain much about "the Kingdom." He assumed that the people already knew. (There was evident confusion among the disciples about whether He meant an earthly, temporal and military kingdom or a spiritual and heavenly one. I find it interesting that Jesus never answered the question clearly enough to eliminate that confusion. Although we would be careful to do so today, apparently Jesus was not afraid of the discrepancy. Note to self: Remember that Jesus allowed His listeners to figure things out for themselves. Even when they got it wrong.)

Even before Jesus' time, Daniel prophesied about a new era: "In the time of those kings, the God of heaven will set up a kingdom that will never be destroyed, nor will it be left to another people. It will crush all those kingdoms and bring them to an end, but it will itself endure forever." (Daniel 2:44). Galatians 1:4 references "this present evil age," while Ephesians 1:21 talks about "the age to come."

There was an understanding that in a future time God Himself would come and sweep away all the earthly powers and establish His reign forever. Jesus had the audacity to proclaim that this Kingdom had arrived with His coming and was now present, and He proceeded to demonstrate it, with power.

What does His Kingdom look like?

Exactly what is the Kingdom that Jesus brought? What characterized it? What did it – *does* it – look like?

The Book of Revelation gives us a clue:

> They will be his people, and God himself will be with them
> and be their God. He will wipe every tear from their eyes.
> There will be no more death or mourning or crying or pain,
> for the old order of things has passed away. (21:3b-4)

The characteristics of the Kingdom of God described by Jesus
are actually the characteristics of heaven. It is the Kingdom of
Heaven that Jesus brings to break into our earthly kingdom. In
God's kingdom, there is no pain, no sickness, no sadness, no
crying, no emotional hurt, no illness, no death, no darkness...the
list goes on almost endlessly. We can imagine it. Or maybe we
can't. It's the best of all possible worlds. Jesus brings that
Kingdom with Him, right into our hearts and into our lives.

Or so He says. But it often doesn't seem that way. In my world
there's plenty of sickness, death, pain, sorrow, crying, darkness,
evil, betrayal, loss, lack, and suffering. I suspect it's the same in
your world too. Where is this Kingdom Jesus speaks of? Who's
in charge here?

There's a short answer and I don't like it. The enemy is in charge
here. God created and put a Kingdom in motion. With the Fall,
Satan gained rulership. There's a reason he's called "prince of
this world" in John 12:31, "god of this world" in 1 Corinthians
4:3-4 and 1 John 5:19, and "ruler of the kingdom of the air" in
Ephesians 2:2.

How do we reconcile those two concepts? Jesus did indeed
bring God's Kingdom to invade this world, and He gave us
authority in the Kingdom as His children and His Bride. As
Christians, we are part of the invading force of Heaven. Before
we take this point too far, remember that it is not unlimited
authority. We cannot simply make happen whatever we want,
need, or desire, even if it is good and with a godly motive; we
are ambassadors who must function within God's intentions
and orders. However, when we do what the Spirit shows us to

do, He does indeed bring freedom, healing, sight, good news, and favor (as Jesus quotes Isaiah in Luke 4:18).

We are in a battleground. We know that He wins in the end, which means we also win in the end. We can't always see that victory now, but we do see glimpses.

We see those glimpses, and even long views, when we recognize clearly what the Father is doing and we pray or act on only that. We see victories when we cooperate with the Kingdom of Heaven as it is invading earth—on His timetable. That's why we pray, "Your kingdom come; Your will be done on earth as it is in Heaven." It's His kingdom that is active, His will that we want to see. As we discover that will and *do* it, we will see the invasion have effect, and increasingly, win.

What do those glimpses look like? They look like the Kingdom of Heaven, which is totally unlike the kingdom we live in. We should see signs and wonders as Heaven invades earth. We should see all manner of miraculous activity, including the sick healed (in heaven no sickness exists); demons cast out (in heaven all evil is destroyed); multiplied food and resources (in heaven there is abundance); the dead raised (in heaven death is destroyed); and even the quelling of the wrath of nature (the wind and waves responded to the authority of Jesus).

And who does these things? God does—through us. The process of ushering in the Kingdom simply cannot end with Jesus' death. After all, He sent out the twelve telling them to heal the sick, raise the dead, and drive out demons (Luke 7). Then, Jesus sent out seventy-two more unnamed followers to do the same thing (Luke 9). With little instruction except what they had seen Jesus do, they did what He commanded and it worked.

Not only did it work, it worked *before both Calvary and Pentecost*!

This was not a group of Christians declaring the death and resurrection life of Jesus. They did not even proclaim the blood of Jesus; after all, He hadn't died yet and the Holy Spirit had not been sent to the church; nor had Jesus breathed on them to receive the Holy Spirit.

Of course, today we realize theologically that His death extended both forward to the end of time and backward to the beginning of creation, establishing His rule and reign and the salvation He so freely gives us. The Holy Spirit was alive in Him and active for all time. But, back then? They weren't "standing on the Scriptures" or relying on promises they had read in their quiet time. They were seventy-two followers, many uneducated fishermen, shepherds, or laborers, who simply did what He told them to do, with His authority and in His name. That's all they had to go on.

This is all He asks us to go on. We are called to do the same thing. He tells us in Matthew 28 to go and do likewise. Fortunately, we have the advantage of the Holy Spirit's equipping and sending as promised in John 14. The Great Commission is a command to go out with His authority, making disciples, and teaching them all He taught. We have no more excuses. We are expected to do exactly what He did, the same things the twelve and the seventy-two did, along with all of the believers in the first churches. This is the foundational expectation of everything Jesus taught: *Go*, and bring the Kingdom of Heaven with you.

Ambassadors

"We are therefore Christ's ambassadors, as though God were making his appeal through us." (2 Corinthians 5:20)

By whose authority do we "go" and do these strange deeds that Jesus did? Is it unlimited authority? Does the commission Jesus gives us presume unlimited power and the ability to do anything we see in Scripture, any time and anywhere?

Jesus expects us to be His ambassadors. Paul calls himself an "ambassador of Christ" in Ephesians 6:20, and in 2 Corinthians he mentions "our" ambassadorship in the context of reconciliation. We are to proclaim the message of God's reconciliation. Not bound any longer by the pain and hurt and sin of this world, we are free to live in Him and He in us. Just as Jesus demonstrated that freedom by signs and wonders, He gives us the power to do the same thing. The activity of the Holy Spirit not only authenticated Jesus' ministry, it accompanies ours.

With one caveat... it's on His terms, not ours.

What are His terms? He gives us authority to do what He tells us to do. An ambassador never speaks on his or her own authority; but when he or she *does* speak, it is with the full authority of the government he or she represents. As ambassadors of the Kingdom of God, we take the authority of the Kingdom everywhere we go. We represent it and we have its authority. Everywhere. The gas station. The bank. The office. Our commute (uh-oh). The meeting with the boss. The meeting with the principal. The line at the grocery store and the time on hold with the cell phone company. Everywhere.

Because Jesus is invading this world every day and because we take bits of the Kingdom of God with us, we should see the same things happening in our lives that Jesus saw and did.

We heal the sick. We encourage. We drive out demons. We bring life where there is death and hopelessness. Some of us may even see the dead raised to life. It can – and does – happen. We should expect it. Why? Because the same life we have received and experienced in worship, prayer, healing, and the presence of God is the life we have the authority to give away...as He tells us where to give it and what to do.

"As" is a crucial preposition. Our authority is conditional.

Now to be fair, I have to address two different groups of Christians. I know them both well; I've been part of them both and still am. They respond to these concepts in totally different ways.

Some of you are seriously scared to think about presuming to know the will of God, or to hear His voice, or to do anything with what you might hear. You want this so badly you can taste it. But you just don't know if you'll ever have the freedom, the "intestinal fortitude," to step out and try anything like healing in Jesus name. To you, it seems entirely presumptuous to speak to conditions, to pray anything remotely like Jesus' prayers of command to "be healed." Worse yet, some paragraphs back I mentioned the grocery store. "Does she mean we have to pray in the grocery store?" you whispered. "With authority, as if we know what God wants us to do? As if WE can do anything! AAAAAAARGH!"

We have more authority than you may think, but first you must take a risk. We've been talking about listening and praying what you hear. Now ask God to speak through your intuition. You have the ability to hear Him. Listen in a new way. Believe that He wants to tell you what He is doing and to give you authority to pray. You don't need to beg. You don't need to plead. There are times for intercession, for begging and pleading and asking God to work. Those are necessary times, and even more so when you're truly desperate. But this isn't time for intercession. This is time for something different.

Once you are actually *with* someone, praying for him or her, there's much more you can do.

You can actively *minister to* the sick, the broken, the lonely, the hurting, or the cashier at the supermarket. By ministering, I mean "speaking to" conditions, saying things that Jesus said, with His authority (more on that later). First of all, *listen*. Know that He wants to speak to you more than you want to listen, and the job of the Holy Spirit is to tell you what to pray. If He tells you what to pray, how much more does He give you the authority to pray it? Try it. You won't be disappointed. When you do get used to praying this way, it will change your life. You'll see what I mean in the next chapter.

Others of you are in a second group. You think you already know what God wants and have practiced this for years. You know all those incredible principles of Scripture and can pray them ALL over ANYONE at a moment's notice. You are eager and ready to war on behalf of your hurting brothers and sisters who are harassed by the enemy. You want desperately to declare healing because you know that all healing has been bought by Jesus' blood on the cross, that all healing is in the atonement, and that only faith allows us to appropriate that healing.

Those of you in this second group...come closer for a moment. I want to whisper a question in your ear: *"Have you asked Jesus whether what you're about to pray is the right thing to pray for that person?"* Say what? You say you want to see the enemy defeated and the person victorious? So do I. I want that person healed and whole. Permanently. Now.

But when you are in a prayer situation, guard against presumption, against immediately praying Scriptures and declarations of healing. Slow down. Listen. Take a minute and ask the Lord what He wants to do for that person, right now. Then speak or pray only what He shows you, in an active voice the way Jesus did, as if He is doing it, which He is, through you. That and no more. I know it's hard. You've been taught to pray anything and everything that you find in Scripture, but just try this for a few days or a month. See what happens.

Then ask the people you prayed for what worked. Did they get better? Were they feeling great the next day? Did healing endure and prosper? What really "clicked" with them? If the prayer was effective, catalogue it in your mental list of "that was God's voice."

Think about it. After He prayed, Jesus asked the blind man in Mark 8 "Do you see anything?" Even Jesus asked, and it did not imply that His prayer was ineffective. To the contrary, He couldn't hold back the flood of those who were healed and had their lives permanently, marvelously, incredibly impacted by the Father. He only did what He saw the Father doing.

No matter what group we find ourselves in, no matter how we are accustomed to praying, we are left with the same conclusion: As ambassadors of the Lord's Kingdom, we only have authority to do what the Father is doing. We need to check in with the home office. Jesus did. We must, too.

Ambassadors do what the Father asks them to do. No more, no less. That is the basis to understand all of the ministry of Jesus and the basis to understand all healing ministry. We do only what He tells us to do in the moment.

Now let's look at what He's accomplished and what part we can play in the drama; or the war, depending on how you look at it.

The Battle

Jesus came to break the kingdom of darkness and by His crucifixion and resurrection He destroyed Satan's grip. We are in a battle in which God is taking back His people from the territory of the enemy. We're enlisted in that army. Although Satan is still in charge, his hold is broken and his fate is secured. Our job is to walk through and fight through the rest of the battles, as Jesus leads and directs us. He is, after all, our Commander in Chief.

Here's an analogy from World War II. We know in retrospect that Hitler was actually defeated on D-Day when the tide of the war turned – the outcome after D-Day was never in doubt. But their victory certainly wasn't obvious to the men on Omaha Beach.

My father was one of those men. He was in the second wave, just after most of the commanding officers were killed in the first wave. H-hour plus 15 minutes. As he told it later, he took the hill and "wiped out a German machine gun nest" by throwing a well-placed grenade. His men got through, some of the first soldiers to do so. But he paid a nasty price. He was shot and left for dead on Omaha Beach. Fortunately, he wasn't dead. He survived to be wounded twice more; was sent home to recuperate, settled into the mundane life of an accountant, and had a daughter nine years later.

My dad couldn't know the outcome when he was on that beach. He did what he needed to do and helped procure freedom. But the war wasn't over yet. So it is with the Kingdom of God; it is "already but not yet."

When we pray, "Thy kingdom come," we are praying for God's rule and reign where there is no sickness, death, or lack. When we see signs and wonders, we see the Kingdom of God breaking into this present age with the ministry of Jesus. He has invaded our lives with His rule and reign. This is where we see battles played out and fought every day. And it's where, sometimes, we see victory.

We live in the "Omaha Beach" days, the in-between times, between the coming of Jesus and the final destruction of Satan at the end of the age. Then, creation will be restored to its original sinless state and the heavenly "no pain and no tears" will be a reality all of the time. Until then, we are in the "present but not yet." We look for it, we long for it, we pray for it, we fight for it, and sometimes we see God's breakthrough. We see it…when we do what the Father is doing.

Healing as Spiritual Warfare – a Broader Context

For many Christians, spiritual warfare connotes violence done to the kingdom of the enemy. To many it seems it must involve loud words, loud voices, and lots of confrontation. That can, indeed, be an aspect of warfare. However, we need to broaden our concept of spiritual warfare.

The warfare that Jesus modeled more often looked like loving the unlovable, healing the broken, and respecting and helping the weak and poor. **We tend to forget that the primary weapon of warfare is *love*.** Going even further, it is healing the sick, soothing the anxious, freeing the oppressed, and comforting those who mourn. It is healing the abused, forgiving those who have wronged, and reconciling the estranged. That, in actuality, is the work of prayer ministry and inner healing and it reclaims territory just as much, or more, than direct attacks against the enemy.

So we find that healing encompasses a great deal more than praying for a broken arm, a bad back, and a suffering heart. Since God is establishing His Kingdom and setting us free from the dominion of sin, death, hell, and the enemy, all of God's work is about restoration and healing. He restores us to right relationship with Him, and therefore with ourselves, and we then see ourselves rightly.

What do I mean by seeing ourselves rightly? Seeing ourselves the way He does, with joy, delight, hope, and encouragement, not with judgment, criticism, exhortation, or comparison. Keep this in mind: You are not God's latest project. He is not a divine tinkerer, never satisfied and always looking to change just one more thing. He made us for relationship, not for improvement.

True healing always leads to restoration of that divine relationship with Him.

What kinds of healing do we see? What are the evidences of the Kingdom of God breaking through to our world and changing us? Here are a few:

- Healing the Spirit — the spiritual self and salvation
- Healing the Body — the physical self
- Healing Past Hurts — the emotional self
- Healing Relationships — forgiveness and reconciliation
- Healing the Demonized — freeing from Satan's power
- Healing the Dead — resuscitation or resurrection

We are all whole, integrated people — body, soul, and spirit. Sickness or disease in one area can impact other areas. It's sometimes not clear which area is the root that causes problems in other areas. But "healing" can involve anything from changing a mental pattern or idea to raising the dead, and everything in between.

One quick note about healing the dead. We don't often hear about this one, but it *is* part of the Biblical model and a definite demonstration of the Kingdom of God. Jesus said in Matthew 10, "As you go, preach this message: 'The kingdom of heaven is near.' Heal the sick, raise the dead, cleanse those who have leprosy, drive out demons."

Years ago, a young Vineyard pastor was praying about why he didn't see resurrections. The Lord responded, "How many dead people are you hanging around with?" A bit taken aback, the pastor joined an EMT squad in order to be where dead people were. The EMTs would work to resuscitate the victim and the pastor would pray, speaking life to the dead body. You might think this would cause a bit of conflict. However, the EMTs had no problem with it; the pastor was fighting death just like they were. He was doing it differently, but they were all on the same team.

How do we know what to pray and what will be effective? Often the Lord will show us surprising ways to pray. Because we are integrated people, the physical, the emotional and the spiritual may all overlap; our prayers may cover any or all of these spheres. Medical science is discovering that emotional pain and trauma contribute to more and more illnesses. Healing in any one area may resolve issues in other areas. Emotional healing may resolve a previously intractable illness. Physical healing may lift the veil of depression or anxiety. We need to keep a holistic view and recognize the interconnectedness of our bodies, minds, emotions and spirit. We may be surprised at the causes and effects we find when we pray.

How do we pray when we've listened? That is where this book becomes practical. We need to have lots of tools in our tool belt so that we can be more effective. We need to learn which tools to use in which situation. "If the only tool you have is a hammer, every problem looks like a nail," said Abraham Maslow. I really don't want to use a hammer if I don't need to. We must use the right tool to be effective. When we teach inner healing, the healing of our emotional selves and the healing of memories, we often say, somewhat facetiously, "You can't inner heal a demon and you can't cast out a memory." A bit overstated, perhaps, but it makes the point: we need to find out just how Jesus did His ministry effectively and how He can work most effectively through us.

Chapter Twelve
Doing What the Father is Doing: Authority to Pray

The pastor prayed passionately for his friend who was quite ill. "Oh Lord," he interceded for the sick person in front of him, "if it be Your will, please heal my friend. And Lord, if it isn't Your will, then would You bring him comfort and peace? And strength to endure? Oh Lord, would You help him cope with this illness?" He went on at length, asking for God's care during this trial. On the face of it, there is nothing wrong with that prayer, but why did the pastor presume it was not God's will to heal? He prayed far more for comfort than healing. Had he asked? Had it even occurred to him that God might be willing – and able – to heal? That God might want to use him – a lowly pastor – to do such a thing? If it was the will of the Father to heal, would the pastor have known it? And would he have known what to pray?

And more importantly, is this how Jesus did it? Is this how He ministered healing?

Oh my, there is much more to this praying business than we thought.

If our purpose is to pray like Jesus, we need to look closely at what He did. When He prayed for people, did He intercede ("Oh Father, would You please heal this son of Yours")? Did He rehearse God's pattern of healing in the past ("Oh Father, I know that You heal, and that it is Your will, just as we see in Scripture...")?[11]

When Jesus ministered, how did He pray? What was His ministry style?

Jesus was not passive. He did not intercede for those who were asking for help unless He was explicitly interceding for those who were not present to Him or involved in the situation. He did intercede aloud once, in the "high priestly prayer" in John 17. There, He prays for Himself, His disciples, and for us – all of those yet to come. That's the time He intercedes.

In every other example we see, He explicitly speaks to the situation at hand. Directly. Without qualification or explanation or hesitation. He tells the centurion in Matthew 8 that his servant has been healed, at a distance, because of the man's faith. Even in that instance, when the servant is nowhere near him, Jesus does not intercede.

Matthew 8 gives us more basis to understand Jesus' ministry. In verses 8 and 9, the centurion explains that he is a man under authority, so he understands the dynamics of command. He knows that if Jesus declares a word, it will be done. The reference to authority astounds Jesus and He commends the centurion—a Roman, an unbeliever, not a Jew—and affirms him for understanding faith.

In Matthew 8:14, Jesus simply touches the hand of Peter's mother-in-law and the fever leaves her.

Yet further, in Matthew 8:23-27, the disciples are afraid when a storm threatens to swamp their boat. He awakes and rebukes

---

[11] He did once. He qualified what He was doing when He prayed to the Father before raising Lazarus. He explained that His prayer to the Father was for the benefit of those who were watching - more explanation than prayer. (John 11:41)

them, "You of little faith, why are you so afraid?", and then commands the winds and waves to be still. Understandably, the disciples are amazed and ask what kind of man this must be that even winds and waves obey him.

And finally, in verses 16 and 32, Jesus calmly drives out spirits (demons) with a word, restoring sufferers to health and sanity.

Clearly, Jesus is trying to show us something. Authority must figure in this equation.

Winds, waves, illnesses, paralysis, and demons all submit to the authority of Jesus. But is it because He is God? Well, yes. But no. (We've been here before, haven't we?) It is because He is a man under the authority of His Father, God, because He sees what the Father is doing and is committed to doing that, and so has the authority to do it.

Think about that for a moment. The Father gives authority to Jesus to do...whatever the Father shows Him to do. By extension then, the Father gives *us* the authority to do what He is doing. If you cannot believe that, let us at least agree that as we pray "in Jesus' name," it is in His authority. Again, we may do only do in His authority what we see Him doing.

But can we believe it? Can we believe that the Father in heaven desires this for us? That He wants not only to answer our cries but to use us in each other's lives in order to "do" those answers?

In Luke 18:8, Jesus ends the story of the begging widow and the unjust judge by assuring us that the Father in heaven is far more willing to answer than the unjust judge, that He will hear and bring about justice quickly for His children. Then He concludes with a question: "When the Son of man comes, will He find faith in the earth?" Jesus wants to know if we have faith to believe that God can do this.

It's not faith in healing that Jesus wants us to have. It's not faith in a formula or a set of words; it's faith in *Him*. It's faith to believe that the Father who loves us will answer quickly. If Matthew 8 and Luke 10 (the sending out of the seventy-two) are any indication, Jesus wants us to have faith to believe that He gives us the same authority that He has.

Our Authority? Or His?

Having seen Christ's authority exhibited boldly, how much of that is available to us? The Scriptures are abundantly clear: Jesus Christ, and His power and authority, live in us. Romans, 1 John, and Colossians all share variations of the same assertion:

> And if the Spirit of him who raised Jesus from the dead is living in you, he who raised Christ from the dead will also give life to your mortal bodies through his Spirit, who lives in you. (Romans 8:11)

> You, dear children, are from God and have overcome them, because the one who is in you is greater than the one who is in the world. (1 John 4:4)

> We know that we live in him and he in us, because he has given us of his Spirit. And we have seen and testify that the Father has sent his Son to be the Savior of the world. If anyone acknowledges that Jesus is the Son of God, God lives in him and he in God. (1 John 4:14-15)

> For God was pleased to have all his fullness dwell in him, and through him to reconcile to himself all things, whether things on earth or things in heaven, by making peace through his blood, shed on the cross. (Colossians 1:19-20)

And, in case we are not convinced,

> For in Christ all the fullness of the Deity lives in bodily form, and you have been given fullness in Christ, who is the head over every power and authority. (Colossians 2:9-10)

My purpose is that they may be encouraged in heart and united in love, so that they may have the full riches of complete understanding, in order that they may know the mystery of God, namely, Christ, in whom are hidden all the treasures of wisdom and knowledge. (Colossians 2:2-3)

Presumption and Passivity

As ambassadors, we now see that we have authority. Christ's authority. God's authority. It's a relatively easy concept to grasp. Except in churches. We church folk can easily fall into either of two extremes, because this truth needs to be qualified.

In some more overtly "charismatic" circles, the tendency is to act as if our authority in Christ means that we can declare anything, any time, because we have His authority, and His willingness to heal and meet our needs has already been assured in Scripture. Without balance, that can be an extreme and unbiblical stance. We do not have unlimited authority to do anything we want. Otherwise, we would all be driving Bentleys or Porsches; or more altruistically, we would empty hospitals with just one word of healing.

At the other extreme, "evangelicals" are more likely to pray mild intercessory prayers ("Oh God, please help Susan to feel better.") because we do not want to be presumptuous. That's not a bad prayer, but it is, in many ways, equally unbiblical. **SHOCK** Really? Well, if we are trying to pray the way Jesus did, then, yes, it is unbiblical. He simply didn't do it that way.

How do we avoid either extreme? At the risk of endless repetition, we do only what we see the Father doing and we do it *boldly*.

The Active Voice

We've already seen that Jesus acted. He spoke. He used either an action or an active voice; a voice of command (and, by the way, the disciples acted similarly in Acts). The Gospels are full of examples. Read through a Gospel and see for yourself. Thumb through Mark, for example. Is this a model we can appropriate for our ministry?

> He took her by the hand and said to her, "Talitha koum!" (which means, "Little girl, I say to you, get up!"). Immediately the girl stood up and walked around (she was twelve years old). At this they were completely astonished. (Mark 5:41-42)

> After he took him aside, away from the crowd, Jesus put his fingers into the man's ears. Then he spit and touched the man's tongue. He looked up to heaven and with a deep sigh said to him, "Ephphatha!" (which means, "Be opened!"). At this, the man's ears were opened, his tongue was loosened and he began to speak plainly. (Mark 7:33-35)

> They came to Bethsaida, and some people brought a blind man and begged Jesus to touch him. He took the blind man by the hand and led him outside the village. When he had spit on the man's eyes and put his hands on him, Jesus asked, "Do you see anything?" He looked up and said, "I see people; they look like trees walking around." Once more Jesus put his hands on the man's eyes. Then his eyes were opened, his sight was restored, and he saw everything clearly (Mark 8:22-25)

> When Jesus saw that a crowd was running to the scene, he rebuked the evil spirit. "You deaf and mute spirit," he said, "I command you, come out of him and never enter him again." (Mark 9:25)

Jesus simply tells Bartimaeus to go after he has declared faith. Jesus uses the active voice to tell him:

"Go," said Jesus, "your faith has healed you." Immediately he received his sight and followed Jesus along the road. (Mark 10:52)

Not only did Jesus use the active voice, but the prophets did as well, releasing what God had shown them and taking authority. When they spoke, they brought into reality what had only been in the heart of God. Elijah declared that the rain would stop and it stopped; He spoke again and the rains came (1 Kings 17-18).

Today, the prophetic person sees what the Father is doing, speaks it into existence, and things happen that weren't imagined before.

In all cases, whether with Jesus, the prophets, the disciples, or us, the principle is the same: the action of the Lord is seen or heard, it is spoken with authority and, empowered by the Father, it happens.

Sounds Like...

What does the active voice sound like? It is direct and authoritative. Here are some examples of prayers of command in the active voice:

- I release you from trying to fix it yourself
- I break the cycle of frenzy and activity
- I speak the peace of Jesus to your body, to your spirit
- In Jesus' name, you are forgiven
- I wash you free from your sin (after prayers of confession and forgiveness)
- I take out of your heart the blackness and replace it with light
- I speak healing and wholeness to your back

- Pain, be gone in Jesus' name (or I command pain to leave…)
- I tell sickness to leave in Jesus' name
- I command muscles to relax in Jesus' name
- I break tension from around your heart
- I lift the burden of responsibility off your shoulders

The first time I heard spoken prayers of command I was horrified. "In Jesus' name I tell this back to be healed," my friend prayed for her husband. I didn't say anything. I didn't want to offend her, but I could not believe her prayers were anything other than extreme presumption. And ineffective, too. "What arrogance," I thought. It took several years before I was comfortable even *hearing* such prayers, let alone speaking them. I needed to understand the theology, know my authority in Jesus, see the prayers work, and just get used to this new concept. It took awhile. A. Long. While. The journey was definitely up hill. But the view from the top was amazing.

The Active Voice, Illustrated

In 1986, I was riding in the passenger seat of our car and Phil was driving. We were on a steep learning curve about ministry and praying the way Jesus did, and it was starting to infect our lives. Healing prayer was always in the back (or front) of my mind.

"I have a headache," Phil interrupted my reverie. Oh no, I thought, that means he'll want me to pray. I was not always the most willing student in the world. He asked, "Would you pray for me?" Just as I expected. I sighed, reached over to put my hand on his forehead, and told him to keep his eyes open while he drove and I prayed. I didn't want to die while praying for a headache.

And then I began a fairly panicked variation of the "Oh God, help" prayer. Only this time I simply fumed at God in my mind. It was not a dialogue; it was a pure rant. The monologue went something like this:

"Well, Lord, I knew he would ask me to do this. I'm stuck in the car and I can't get out. It won't look good if I say no. I *can't* say no. So I'm going to pray. But You and I know that nothing is going to happen. Maybe You do this through other people but You don't do it through me. I'm being obedient because I have no choice. But You and I both know it won't work." The only thing I did not do was stick out my lower lip and pout.

I prayed with absolutely no faith or expectation that the headache would go away but I prayed the way I had been taught. I prayed the only words that seemed appropriate at the moment, the only phrases that came to mind. I simply spoke to the pain and the headache and told them to go away in Jesus' name. I still remember every word:

"Holy Spirit, come. Show me how to pray. (Pause for deep breath and try to listen but am too panicked to hear much.) In Jesus' name, I speak to the pain and tell it to go and I tell the headache to go. And I tell the muscles to be relaxed and the blood pressure to go down. Holy Spirit, come and fill Phil and every place that the pain was. In Jesus' Name, Amen."

Good, that was done. It was all I could think of. Humiliated, I slunk lower in my seat and looked out the window. "Thanks, it's gone," Phil said simply and continued driving.

"WHAT??? WHAT???" I was listening now. "It's gone," he repeated. It took a while to sink in. IT WORKED! GREAT!!! Wait, not great. Surprisingly, I was not elated. Oh, I was glad the pain was gone, but success could mean only one thing: He'd ask me to pray AGAIN the next time he had a headache. This was proving to be quite the awkward journey. How stupid did it look to be *speaking* to *headaches*?

For about six months, Phil called me "the headache lady." God was laughing. Every time I prayed for headaches and dared to use the active voice, the headaches would leave. Anyone's headaches would leave. It didn't matter who it was. Every time I prayed, I knew I'd have to speak to the headache. I was getting awfully used to looking stupid. But somewhere along the way, I learned. When God tells me to do something, I need to *do* it, not ask *Him* to do it, because He's given me the authority to do it in His name.

Ministry or Intercession? A Diagram

How do we do this? What does it look like?

There seem to be at least four forms of prayer in Scripture. For those of us who are more linear and need a picture, the models of prayer look like this:[12]

God
↑
1) Praise and worship   us

God
↑↓
2) Petition   us

God
↑ ↘
3) Intercession   us   person

---

[12] From ministry training at Vineyard Christian Fellowship, New Haven, CT 1986; unpublished notes by Bill Elander and Joe Paskewich.

4) Prayer Ministry us ➜ person

In the first form above, we worship and adore God. The direction is from us to Him.

In Petition, we ask God to *please* help us. (The famous seven-word prayer again: "Oh God, oh God, oh God, HELP!") The direction is from us to God, and (we hope) back to us as He answers our plea.

In Intercession, the direction is from us…to God…to the person who needs His intervention. "Oh God, please help him!" we pray.

But in this last form of prayer, which we call "Prayer Ministry" because we actively "minister" to the person as Jesus did, we are actually the *agent* of God. We are not merely an *instrument* of God, passively waiting for Him to use us. Instead, we actively hear and do what the Father is doing. We *assume* that God's authority is in us and He *wants*, in *every* situation, to use us in some way.

Remember, He gave authority to the twelve, then to the seventy-two, and then to us. He wants us to go with equipment, part of which is the knowledge and ability to use our words creatively, to take authority where *He has already given it.*

A Parable...

A child and his father have a regular routine. The dad and the son walk out of their door, down the front walk, down the sidewalk, and go one whole block down the street. They stop at the corner and go into the candy store.

It's a small town and the friendly man behind the counter smiles at the little boy who stares up at the trays and bins of candy in the glass case. He looks up at his father and Dad nods. They are used to this routine. "Yes, you may have peanut butter cups," Dad says, "Two?" The boy nods. Dad looks over to the man behind the counter. "Two peanut butter cups, please, in a bag."

"That will be eighty-nine cents, sir," says the merchant, and the bag is in the child's hands.

Soon, the child is old enough to venture down the block by himself. There are no streets to cross and Dad is confident in his son's ability. One day the child asks, "Daddy, can we go to the store and get peanut butter cups?"

The Dad thinks for a moment. "Well, son, I think you're old enough to do this yourself." The son's eyes grow rather large but he listens. "I'll give you the money and I want you to go to the store today on your own. Can you do that?"

The son takes the eighty-nine-cents and slowly walks to the street. It looks bigger and scarier without Dad but he walks slowly down the block. Suddenly, he is very aware of the houses, the people, the cars. "What if..." The question is unfinished, but the damage is done. He turns and runs as fast as he can back to the front porch, only to find his Dad waiting on the step, watching. "Did you get the candy?" Dad asks.

But the son can only hide in His father's arms. "Daddy, will you take me to the candy store," he pleads.

"No, son, you can do this. I gave you the money. You'll be fine. Just go out the door, turn right, go down the street, and give the money to the man behind the counter. He will give you the peanut butter cups. You can do this!"

The little boy tries again. This time he gets all the way to the corner, but the door of the store looms big, dark and *scary*. Once again he runs home.

And once again, his father reassures him and sends him to the store. The son tries one more time, still unsure, looking bravely up at the big glass door staring down at him. Can he really do this? Is it safe? Will the man give him the candy? Why won't Daddy come with him? The task seems impossibly large and the son feels...Very Small.

We are so like that child, you and I. We desperately want the candy, but we are convinced that we aren't allowed to buy it. Forgetting that the Father has given us the money for precisely this purpose and has instructed us to go to the store to buy it, we run home and ask Daddy to buy it for us.

"No," He says gently as he nudges us out the door. "I've given you the money. You can do this."

You already have the money. Now take the authority. Like it or not, there's a difference between intercession, asking the Father to buy the candy, and ministry, buying it ourselves with His permission and His money. Each approach has its place, but one is for a different purpose than the other.

...And a Story

I was not feeling well. The symptoms did not look good. Mild fever, scratchy throat, hints of chills, a budding illness. "Would you pray for me?" I asked my husband. He agreed and began to intercede. He interceded. And interceded passionately some more. Through the whole prayer, I found myself thinking, "Just speak to the virus. Curse the virus." Oh dear. It's not effective for the pray-ee to be the pray-er at the same time. I waited, hoping he'd hear the same thing. He didn't.

Finally, I opened my eyes and whimpered, "Just speak to the virus. Curse it in Jesus' name." It's mightily inconvenient to be so comfortable training others in healing prayer. Sometimes it leaks out in the most awkward ways.

Phil protested, "But I don't know if that's what I should pray." My patience was wearing thin and the fever was not helping. I was cranky. "Well, I do, so just do it!" I snapped. Poor Phil. But, blessedly, he did it.

And I felt better.

I hate it when that happens. No, I mean, I *love* it when *healing* happens, but why does one form of prayer "work" and another "not work?" Because that's how authority functions. Boldly. We act on what we have heard because God has handed us the "money," the faith-filled currency of healing.

What do we have authority over? What do we *not*?

What do we have authority over? The short answer is this: We have authority over what Jesus demonstrated that *He* had authority over when He was walking the earth: illnesses, demons, nature, the world, our families, our friends, and our property. The physical and spiritual things that directly affect us. The people we love and the ones we pray for.

He healed illnesses, rebuked evil spirits and fevers, cast out demons, raised the dead, and commanded the winds. He spoke to situations, conditions, nature, people, and spirits. So do we. Or at least, we should.

There is not a lot of evidence in Scripture, at least not directly, that we have authority over anything in the heavenlies. There may be some arguments from indirect implications and Old Testament analogies, but we have no direct model from Jesus for anything more than authority over our earthly realm. Taking authority over principalities and powers and territorial spirits is, at best, controversial. It may be downright dangerous.[13] In any case, we have plenty to do in this realm to keep us busy for a very long time. We have a long way to go just in the realms of sickness, dysfunction, and death.

Our challenge is this: If He's showed us something, we need to do it. At the very least, we must ask Him what to do with what we've sensed, seen, tasted, smelled, or thought.

Then we must take a deep breath…and take a chance.

If He has shown us what to do, then He has called us to partner with Him, with His authority, as fully equipped ambassadors. We are no less than stealth agents of the Kingdom of God.

---

[13] For a fuller discussion of this concept, See John Paul Jackson's *Needless Casualties of War*, Streams Publications, 1999

*Leadership and
Praying for Others*

Chapter Thirteen
Who Does This?

Prayer ministry is not for a select few saints who have regularly visited heaven! Prayer is something we all can do. We praise Him. We ask God about our lives. We talk with him and intercede for others. And we pray for others in prayer ministry. I do. You do. But in order to learn how to pray, you have to… pray. Put another way, you have to practice.

Praying for others is a learned art. The more you do it, the more comfortable you will be. Remember the pastor's exhortation, "Go pray for a thousand people?" As much as I hated that admonition, it worked. The more people I prayed for, the more I learned.

But paradoxically, one of the best ways to learn to pray is also to *get* prayer. Lots of prayer. Be a prayer "hog." Receive, receive, receive! Everyone who receives has something to give. That which you have faced and which the Lord has conquered in your own life is what you have authority to give away.

Most of us start out in prayer ministry with a passionate desire to help others. I did. Phil did. Virtually every prayer minister I know did. But for most of us, that desire progressed to a profound awareness of our own brokenness. It seems that the Lord does not let us proceed very far down the "helper" path without teaching us what it is to be "helped."

As we face our own pain, dysfunction, and weakness, we develop a deep sensitivity about what is necessary and useful. We see what has worked for us and for those around us as we hobble down a very long road, leaning on the Lord and on our friends. Soon, very soon, we find ourselves praying for others who struggle, helping them as we have been helped.

Praise be to the God and Father of our Lord Jesus Christ, the Father of compassion and the God of all comfort, who comforts us in all our troubles, so that we can comfort those in any trouble with the comfort we ourselves have received from God. (2 Corinthians 1:3-4)

A pastor once told me he chooses leaders by watching who receives prayer. Indeed, the person who is open to receiving is better equipped to give. The one who has faced his or her own pain and sinful tendencies, who has received compassion and mercy, is a safe candidate to offer that same compassion and mercy to another.

The only way to give is to receive first; the only way to pray for another is to learn to receive prayer for yourself. And then, learn to step out and provide a safe place for the weary ones all around you.

Chapter Fourteen
Creating a Safe Space

No one who is wounded wants to walk back into the same firefight from which he just escaped. Instead, he finds a way, whether driven, dragged, carried, or stumbling on his own, to a safe hospital. There he can be bandaged, tended, mended, and nursed back to health.

But what if the hospital is filled with snipers? What if the very ones who are supposed to care are dispensing manuals of instruction and criticism instead of quietly bandaging wounds and providing rest?

One of the primary responsibilities of the pray-er is to create a safe healing environment for the person receiving prayer. Similarly, one of the primary tasks for a small group leader is to create a safe environment for the group's members to share, pray for one another, and encourage each other in love.

Safety is essential in order for someone who wants help to be honest, real, and open with you—and with God. The one you are praying for may have suffered significant harm to his or her image of God. Most of us have. You, as a leader and pray-er, must model for that person the true attitude of Jesus, one of love, care, encouragement, and hope.

Remember that Jesus' primary role now is to sit at the right hand of the Father, interceding on our behalf. He is on our side, seeing us with eyes of faith and favor. That is a task that we can't do for ourselves. But you, as a pray-er, must do it for the one you are caring for.

Here are four primary guidelines[14] that will make you a safe listener and pray-er, and which will keep your prayer sessions and small groups safe and encouraging: Confidentiality, honesty, being personal, and avoiding advice. Without these guidelines, you run the risk of further damaging those who are already suffering, which may drive them away from further help in the future. Some of us are very resilient and come back for prayer anyway. Sadly, most of us do not.

However, with these guidelines your group or prayer time can be a safe place for the person who needs help and a sanctuary that the Holy Spirit can easily fill. Guidelines are like fences; they help set boundaries for you and your team, as well as for the person receiving prayer. They allow you to focus and to give help in the very place it is the most needed.

For those of you who like acronyms, one of our prayer team members recently pointed out that our guidelines form the word C-H-A-P. In 24 years, it had not occurred to us. Actually, the original acronym she discovered was…ahem… C-R-A-P, but we thought that CHAP was a bit less offensive. Either way, you may decide which you prefer.

Confidentiality

The first guideline that Phil and I require in our prayer teams and leaders is confidentiality. It is essential for any healing or counseling ministry. Breaches of confidentiality seriously harm both the victim and the ministry. In secular counseling and medical practice, breaking confidentiality can cost a practitioner his or her job or license to practice. If someone on a prayer team violates this trust knowingly, we recommend that the person be

---

[14] From small group training at VCF New Haven, 1985; adapted from guidelines of various recovery movements and support groups.

removed from prayer teams or support group leadership or, at the very least, be on probation for a significant period of time.

Mandated Reporting

Confidentiality must be absolutely observed except in two situations: if the person requesting help reveals serious, active intent to harm himself or others (suicide, homicide, or abuse) or if there is active child abuse. In either of these cases, the situation must be reported to an authority: the pastor or prayer ministry supervisor, or secular authorities.

If abuse is suspected or has happened recently, or if someone is in danger, it is probably wise to report that as well, but it may not be legally mandated. When you pray for others, you are performing a pastoral function, whether as a lay person or as a clergy person. You are considered a "mandated reporter" and you must report abuse or intent to harm.

What is "active intent" to harm? It's not clearly defined but usually involves current and/or specific plans. Often when a person expresses thoughts of suicide, he or she is looking for attention or help. However, if he or she has made specific plans, that is "active intent." If someone reports purchasing a gun with the specific goal of hurting someone else, that is an indicator of "active intent." It's a good idea to ask gently, "Have you made plans?" Be aware, though, that a seriously suicidal or homicidal individual may be hiding the fact. Their plans are often covert.

Mandated reporting does not apply to "grey areas" in which you are uncomfortable with ethical decisions or sinful behaviors. Those need to be addressed according to the standards of your church or ministry. However, it is wise to know those standards and to address those possibilities *before* you begin praying. You don't want to be mid-prayer and realize that you do not know what to do. In any case, the best strategy is to be as prepared as possible, with a clear support system in place so you know whom to turn to for advice.

In some places and situations, you may be required or advised to undergo training to guard against inappropriate situations and abuse. Although it may seem unnecessary at the time, background screening and abuse prevention training are as much a protection for you as they are tools to spot potential abuse. This is another reason why we always recommend praying in teams of two or more. There is built in protection, safety, and accountability for you, the team, and the person requesting prayer.

You need to know your ministry or church's guidelines for counseling, prayer and safety; you should also know your state guidelines for mandated reporting. Those guidelines are not the same in all areas. If in doubt, check with your supervisor or pastor. If they don't have guidelines in place, or if they do not know their state's mandated reporting laws, a protective system should be implemented as soon as possible. It's one way we stay "wise as serpents and innocent as doves."

Confidentiality sets up a safe environment; the next step is being honest and real.

Honesty (Be Real)

Effective prayer requires honesty. We will probably not receive as much help as we need if we ask for vague or generic prayer or confess large and non-specific faults. "Forgive me for all the things I've ever done," prayed with honesty, actually accomplishes the task of confession. But it's not easy to appropriate the forgiveness God offers for such a broad summary. "Forgive me for shoplifting in ninth grade. Forgive me Lord, for lying and stealing that day" gets a lot more specific. It's also a lot harder to be that real.

It's much more difficult to be open about our pain or to ask for prayer in an environment where we think others are hiding behind safe and distant walls. The more honest we are with each other, the more we can realize the Father's unconditional love and forgiveness. The more we experience God's acceptance, the more we are free to share it with each other. The love and acceptance that we experience with each other and the unconditional love of God gradually disarm and dispel our sense of shame.

We encourage everyone we lead, both in small groups and in prayer situations, to take off masks and to be open with one another. We also do the same things ourselves.

Leadership does not entitle us to hide behind an image of perfection and holiness. Instead, it demands that we be open, vulnerable, and transparent with those we lead. How can we expect honesty in others if we are not prepared to be honest ourselves?

This does not mean that we share our own stories with every person we pray for; in fact, we guard their time very carefully and concentrate on them. But it does mean that we share often in groups or as we teach.

We saw this most clearly a few years ago when we housed several pastors for a seminary course. After hearing about our inner healing series, one of them came to hear us teach. In class, we routinely share stories from our own lives. Most often, those stories are rather intense and revealing because we want participants to feel safe sharing the pain of their own lives. That night was no exception.

Afterwards, the pastor approached us to share his reaction. Knowing that pastors are not usually noted for personal vulnerability in front of their congregations, I was prepared for the worst. I expected him to chastise me for being too transparent. Instead, I was surprised to hear him thank us for our openness. "I thought your authority would be diminished when you shared so vulnerably in front of the class," he said thoughtfully. "I was always taught that leaders shouldn't share that way, so I was watching for the class reaction. That's why I came, to see what would happen. But I was surprised. Instead of reducing your authority, your sharing actually increased it." Wow. That was not what I thought he'd say.

Phil and I had always seen good responses to our vulnerability since it freed people to admit their own weaknesses. Our friend's reaction confirmed and deepened our conviction that leaders need to be real.

If leaders were more authentic, would the wounded people in our congregations find it easier to pursue healing? Our own experiences lead us to believe that they would. Phil and I have been committed to transparency and vulnerability in our leadership for more than 20 years. We've seen the fruit, and it's good.

No Advice

If there is one rule that can create a sense of safety, this is it.

If there is one rule that creates enormous controversy, this is it.

No other concept that we teach has ever generated as much flak as this one small guideline: Please, when listening and praying for others, do not give advice, not even the prophetic, scriptural kind.

Why not? As Christians, aren't we salt and light to the world? Don't we have answers to give? Don't we help others with the lessons we have learned? Yes, yes, and yes. But not in small group sharing and not in prayer.

Why not? (This question is always asked twice. No one gives up easily on the "right" to admonish others.) We don't give advice because it is generally not needed or wanted; because we are not there to "fix" the problem; because it is up to God to point out a person's sin or problem, not up to us; because it absolutely destroys safety and may cause a person to be defensive or to shut down; because the person may do exactly the opposite in response to advice; because the person has probably tried any number of solutions before coming for prayer as a last resort; and (most importantly) almost everyone who asks for advice really doesn't want it.

You read that last line correctly; it is not a typo. Almost all of the people who ask for advice, *even if they insist that they want it,* probably don't. What they really want is encouragement. They want to know that the solution they already thought about will work. They want to discover the answers for themselves. They want to know that there is hope and that God cares, has compassion, and heals. They want to receive God's specific word to them in prayer. They want to be heard and they want affirmation. But they do not want advice.

And they do not want prayers of advice either: "Oh Lord, just teach her that _____." And... "Oh Lord, just show him that_____." (....you fill in the blanks.) And the worst prayers of advice? The scriptural ones: "Oh Lord, just show her Hezekiah 69:10, that if she just..." etc., etc., etc.

Therapy groups and some recovery groups know this guideline well. They don't allow "crosstalk" because of the shame, judgment, and reaction that it can bring. Advice is the fastest way to shut down sharing. It tells me that my feelings are not valid, and puts the advice-giver in a superior, one-up position over me.

Is there anyone still out there? I fear I have just offended every single reader. For those who remain, let me go back in time and explain.

I used to hate this "no-advice" rule. I fought against it for years. Friends and I would tease, "Let's go out behind the barn and give advice," until I realized that all of the extraordinary advice I gave my friends was ignored. Advice ended conversations. All of the wonderful words I had for people in small groups only drove them away. Even the wisdom our teams imparted was routinely ignored, especially by the people who asked for it the most.

Also, I discovered that I, who so lovingly and intensely gave good advice and wisdom all the time, hated advice when it was given to me. Ouch. I realized that it drove me further from the truth that God was speaking to my heart. It stopped me from sharing and kept me locked in my pain. It was then that I realized that all my well-meaning advice was having the same effect on other people.

I went cold-turkey. I stopped. I determined not to give advice. I didn't stop easily, mind you. I sat on my tongue and, honestly, I still do. (My tongue is now very long and flat...)

How freeing it was to discover that my advice didn't matter. Suddenly, I didn't have to have the right answers. I didn't have to share that urgent prophecy right that very minute. I didn't have to "fix" anything. They weren't going to miss God's best plan for them if I didn't speak up. The pray-ees weren't going to destroy their future if I only listened. My advice wasn't going to make or break anything.

Suddenly people were freer to share and freer to receive, and we saw more of God's effective work.

To my surprise, other prayer team members noticed the same thing. People asking for prayer weren't coming for counsel, they were coming for *prayer*. Duh!

Of course, this is not to say that there isn't a place for advice. Let me say that in a positive way: there is definitely a place for advice and counsel. There is a place for teaching. But prayer sessions and small support groups are not that place.

This is why we don't allow our prayer teams to lapse into counseling. This is why we don't call ourselves counselors (although we carry liability insurance in case a few words of advice leak out on occasion). This is why we happily refer people to teachers, counselors, and professional therapists who know how and when to give advice rightly.

Our job (and yours) is:

> to get the person,
>
> and the problem,
>
> and Jesus
>
> in the same room
>
> at the same time
>
> and see what happens.

If you are prone to advice-giving when you listen or pray, try some new ways of responding. When you hear something from the Lord, ask Him what to do with it. When you pray for someone, give plenty of room for him or her to reject or reinterpret what you are praying or saying. Try prefacing your words with "I wonder..." or "Perhaps..." or "Have you thought..." or "I see a picture of..." or "This may not be the Lord, but..." or "I think I'm hearing... Does that make any sense to you?" Let the person draw his or her own conclusion and hear what the Lord wants him or her to do. Prayer appointments are a set-apart sanctuary from the rest of life; they are a time to bless, not a time to fix.

Not to fix? Really? That's especially hard for those of us who know that the Lord wants to bring change and we're fairly sure we know what the change needs to be. We want to provide the answers that the Lord has shown us in the Word or the solutions that we know or have learned. But remember, *we* learned these things for ourselves and the ones we pray for need to do the same thing.

If you remember only two points from this book, remember these:

- **Listen to the Father and do what He is doing; and**

- **Don't give advice. Just get the person, the problem, and Jesus in the same place, at the same time.**

And see what happens!

Be Personal

In many places around the country where we have taught, trained, and led small groups, this is affectionately known as the "no Aunt Maude rule." In your travels, if you hear someone say that you'll know where it came from.

"Be Personal" means talk about *you*. Not your Great Aunt Maude. Not your Great Aunt Maude's cat. Not your Great Aunt Maude's trouble with her cat destroying her house. Tell us about *you*. Now, if your Great Aunt Maude was the only mother you ever knew, and she just died, and you are devastated.... Well, that's a different story. That's about you and how you feel.

We are vitally, passionately, intensely interested in how YOU feel and what you need prayer for. We actually have you in front of us and we want to pray for you. We can lay hands on you, if you want us to—in the best Biblical sense, of course. We can encourage you. We can pray for you. We can love you and care for you. Your Great Aunt Maude is not here so we can't lay hands on her, or her cat. We can, and will, pray for her later, but right now, we care about you. How are YOU doing?

The "be personal" rule applies in one other way: It is not fair for me to sit in a prayer session or a small group and tell others that they need to get prayer. Even if they do. Even if I KNOW they do. *Especially* if I know they do. They need to be responsible for themselves. This a matter of boundaries.

We want to encourage people to get prayer, but they have to ask for themselves. Otherwise, we are encouraging them to remain passive, to hide, and to expect others to read their minds. If they do not ask for themselves, they are also less likely to be able to receive prayer and to engage in the process fully.

It is important to take initiative for oneself and ask for prayer, to be desperate, willing, and tenacious. It seems to make us more open. So take a risk. Be personal, and tell us how YOU are doing. We really want to know.

The real core of all these guidelines for safety is this: we learn to take responsibility for ourselves, not for other people. We care but we do not control. We create a safe space for people to share and to receive prayer. And we leave the result between them and the Lord.

Chapter Fifteen
Preparation for Prayer: Intercession, Fasting, and Protection

Intercession

Perhaps you're one of those precious saints who loves to pray. You have always prayed. You pray for crises, broken marriages, crying colicky babies, and lost puppies. You pray for anointed sermons, inspired teaching, powerful outreach and massive revival. Where, you may ask, is the place for the way you pray? Is intercession banned from prayer ministry sessions? Is this just a new style that will make you feel antique?

Be reassured. There is a place for intercession. There is a time for you to pray the way you're used to. Indeed, you must intercede and cry out for the healing of millions of hurting hearts. We prayer ministers need you to intercede!

But only for one purpose. Preparing the ground.

We intercede when we are not sure what the Father is doing. We intercede when we are home alone, or with two or four or seventy other people, crying out for God to intervene. We intercede in the car on the way to a big meeting and all the time as we walk with the Lord through our days.

In short, we intercede any time we are not praying for someone directly. If the people we're praying for aren't in front of us and we can't lay hands on them, then it's safe to intercede.

In fact, it's essential. The effectiveness of every prayer ministry appointment and every in-person prayer time depends on it.

Intercession is an act of mediation. We come between an individual (or entity) and God and we pray for His help and reconciliation.[15] It involves authority (there's that word again) and delegation. Lawyers mediate all the time. The word is actually not limited to prayer. Jesus' current role is as our intercessor, not necessarily just our Pray-er. He intercedes (intervenes) for us, going before the Father on our behalf.

> But because Jesus lives forever, he has a permanent priesthood. Therefore he is able to save completely those who come to God through him, because he always lives to intercede for them. (Hebrews 7:24)

> For there is one God and one mediator between God and men, the man Christ Jesus. (1 Timothy 2:5)

> My dear children, I write this to you so that you will not sin. But if anybody does sin, we have one who speaks to the Father in our defense—Jesus Christ, the Righteous One. (1 John 2:1)

Intercessory *prayer* is simply an extension of Jesus' work of intercession and is something He wants to do through us. In it we represent Jesus and His work. We are "sent ones" to whom intercession, or intercessory prayer, has been delegated. Again, as with our study in Colossians, we are agents of God. We are representatives with authority so our intercession and our intercessory prayer accomplish much: in essence, in intercessory prayer, as in prayer ministry, we are co-laborers with Jesus.

We pray because we have been told it works and we pray with the right perspective so that it *will* work:

---

[15] For more in-depth discussion on intercession, see Dutch Sheets' book, *Intercessory Prayer*, Regal Books, 1996.

What causes fights and quarrels among you? Don't they come from your desires that battle within you? You want something but don't get it. You kill and covet, but you cannot have what you want. You quarrel and fight. You do not have, because you do not ask God. When you ask, you do not receive, because you ask with wrong motives, that you may spend what you get on your pleasures. (James 4:1-3)

Richard Foster, in his classic work *Celebration of Discipline*, says it this way: "In prayer, real prayer, we begin to think God's thoughts after him: to desire the things he desires, to love the things he loves, to will the things he wills. Progressively, we are taught to see things from His point of view."[16]

And, perhaps most importantly, we pray because Jesus did it – seemingly He *had* to, in order to survive and to meet the demands of ministry. Jesus met with His Father (Mark 1:35); the disciples did the same, as did the early leaders of the church. In Acts 6:4, they set apart deacons so that the apostles and leaders could do the work of "prayer and ministry of the Word." Prayer was their way of doing the work.

If Jesus, the disciples, the apostles, and all the leaders of the church needed to pray in order to minister effectively and to nurture their relationship with the Father, so do we. But it is not a practice born of obligation. Instead, it is born of relationship and it not only enlivens us, but facilitates ministry. We do not have to make this harder than it is.

What about fasting?

Fasting is an expected discipline of the Christian life; it permeated the Hebrew lifestyle as well. Its purpose is not to convince or manipulate God but to open us to more of the work

---

[16] Richard J. Foster, *Celebration of Discipline*, Harper San Francisco, 3rd edition, 1988, p.33.

and wisdom of the Holy Spirit. It is not always possible to adopt fasting as a regular discipline but when it is added the benefits are tangible and potent. Prayer is essential; fasting allows our prayers to fly.

> After Jesus had gone indoors, his disciples asked him privately, "Why couldn't we drive it [the demon] out?" He replied, "This kind can come out only by prayer." (and in some manuscripts: "prayer and fasting") (Mark 9:28-29)

Fasting and prayer prepare the way for what the Father will do. They open and prepare your heart. They open the heart of the prayer team and the person receiving prayer. They make any prayer ministry situation much, much easier. They break down the walls before you actually lay hands on people and pray. The time to intercede is the time when you're home or beforehand with other prayer team members when you're *not* ministering. Then, when you minister in-person, half the job is already done.

That is not to say that one may not "minister" without having fasted or interceded. Not at all. But any ministry is more effective after fasting and prayer.

The more you intercede, the more preparation the Spirit can do in advance. Mark 9:29, above, seems to imply that if you intercede beforehand, then the area is primed in the spiritual realm so that the work of prayer ministry flows more easily. Apparently there are situations in which fasting and (prior) prayer are prerequisites for successful ministry. Often we've found that diseases, wounds and spiritual forces were only "dented" when we ministered without interceding before hand. When we added fasting and intercession to our preparation, those same conditions were healed and the persons we prayed for were significantly changed.

Protection

The enemy is well acquainted with prayer and he does not like it. He is especially upset if he sees Christians taking authority and setting captives free, bringing healing and release and hope to those around them. He would like nothing more than to decommission us, harm us, and take us offline. He does not want us praying and he most certainly does not want us to use the Lord's authority.

Intercessory teams are your first line of offense as well as defense in this spiritual war. They are the faithful ones who pray for you before, during, and after you minister—which is pretty much all the time if you are doing even a small amount of ministry.

A good team of intercessors will help win the battle before you even get to the front lines. Intercession and fasting are like the air attacks before the infantry moves in. They take out as many enemy strongholds as possible so that the army has fewer and easier battles to fight on the ground. Like a defensive shield against the attacks of the enemy, prayer and fasting strengthen your resolve, increase your awareness of God's presence and His voice, sharpen your discernment and blunt the force of the adversary's onslaught.

You also need your own armor. The Ephesians 6:10-18 armor of God is essential. You must know who you are, whose authority you have, whose righteousness you bear, where your salvation comes from, whose truth you believe, and where it comes from. Your Bible, which is God's word for all time, and your sanctified intuition, which leads you to God's application of His word for *right now*, are your two closest friends.

Now, let's take a step back.

Look at you.

You started with an empty tool belt. No, that's not true. Unless I miss my guess, you had intercession all along or you wouldn't be reading this book. But look at your tool belt now. You have more than just a hammer. Your tool belt is full, you have prepared the ground, and you understand your equipment. Now it's time to get started.

Chapter Sixteen
Diagnosis and Prayer Choices

You are about to pray for someone (and by this I mean "prayer ministry," as in "in-person, laying-on-of-hands" kind of ministry. The kind you *don't* do at home alone in your bedroom). You're sweating. You hope the person doesn't notice that you're nervous. You have no idea what to do next. Where do you begin?

The first place to start when you pray for someone is to *listen.* Yes, more listening.

But this time you have to listen to the person who wants prayer. What does he or she want prayer *for*? That is the very first question we ask when we prepare to pray. After all, we don't need to wait for a "word of knowledge" for something that the person can easily tell us!

Then the questions come more easily. What is the presenting problem? What might be underneath that presenting problem and what do they need to do? Is forgiveness an issue? Is this the right time to "go deeper?" Or is that for later? And how much time is available, anyway?

The questions can seem endless, but we only need them to help guide our prayer direction. We listen with one ear toward God and another ear toward the person. Listening to both, we can start to discern where to begin.

However, this is not *only* about listening (whew!). Some practical suggestions can establish the direction and content for prayer. The setting, as well as basic prayer categories, possible root causes, and clarifying questions, all help to direct the ministry time.

The Setting

In our desire to help the people who are asking for prayer, we may forget one crucial and very freeing fact: the setting in which we're praying will have a lot to do with what we—and they—can expect. When I pray for someone after church, I have far less time than when I pray for someone during a pre-arranged two-hour inner healing prayer appointment. Someone who comes to the altar for prayer after a moving sermon may be hoping that every issue and wound will be dealt with in the next five minutes. However, short of a major revival, when things seem to happen almost instantaneously, that is probably unrealistic.

In general, there are probably three settings for prayer, each with its own limitations on length of time and how much can be accomplished.

1) **Prayer on the Street or After a Church Service:**

Available time: About five minutes

Probable content: This will usually be the shortest and most pointed prayer experience. On the street, it may involve a word of knowledge and a quick prayer for healing. At a conference, the same thing might apply. After church, or after the sermon, there is typically time only for a short prayer agreeing with the person's request and encouraging him or her. There is little time for talk and no time for counselling.

What it is not: This is not time for deep inner healing or deliverance. All counseling, and any needs deeper than what can be addressed in a quick 5-minute prayer, should be referred to another setting or an appropriate supervisor, pastor, or counselor.

Strategy: Ask a few concise questions, briefly listen for insight from God, and pray for the person's request or situation as the Lord directs. Primarily, encourage the person you're praying for.

2) **Support group prayer or ministry after topical teaching:** Prayer in a trusted small group or in a small structured setting with a particular focus

Available time: About 15-30 minutes

Probable content: This may involve more in-depth and focused prayer, interview time, consideration of root issues, and possibly some level of inner healing or simple deliverance. The prayer probably focuses on specific requests arising from crises or everyday life. The goal of the prayer time is to help the person cope with and overcome the struggles of daily life.

What it is not: This is not time for deep inner healing or deliverance, which usually requires 1-2 hours or multiple sessions. It is not time for teaching or therapy—remember that you are a prayer minister, not a therapist. It is probably not time for major prophecy concerning life-altering crises. It is "daily-life-support" prayer or prayer about a focused issue. Situations requiring counsel, deep inner healing, deliverance, prophecy for major decisions, "soaking prayer," or multiple sessions should be referred to an appropriate team. Counseling should be referred to an appropriate pastor or counselor.

Strategy: Stress the guidelines for sharing to remind the team or group members about the session boundaries and to reassure the person receiving prayer. Ask questions and get enough information to begin to pray. Concentrate on prayer rather than conversation; listen for the Lord's leading as long as necessary and try to ascertain and deal with root issues when possible.

3) Deep inner healing prayer, soaking prayer, or deliverance:[17]

Available time: 1-2 hours

Probable content: This is time to go as deep as possible. A prepared questionnaire may be helpful to solicit information in advance; the prayer session may involve more in-depth and focused prayer, interview time, consideration of root issues, and some level of inner healing or deliverance. It probably focuses on specific requests arising from counseling, personal crises or everyday life, and is designed to help the person overcome physical issues, wounds from the past and patterns in the present, as well as situations from daily life. Avoid giving advice.

What it is not: This is not a counseling appointment. If the person receiving prayer needs to talk, refer him or her to counseling. It is not primarily a time for intercession but for *ministry*.

Strategy: If possible, fast and pray before the appointment and use a questionaire, if you can, to help direct your intercession and preparation. Reassure the person you're praying for that this is a safe and confidential environment by using the "guidelines for sharing," if necessary. Interview and get as much information as you need but move to prayer as soon as possible. Listen extensively to the Holy Spirit. Attempt to address root causes and issues and check regularly with the person receiving prayer in order to gauge effectiveness and to re-direct prayer. Continually maintain eye contact with the team. Involve the person receiving prayer as much as necessary, especially if he or she needs to confess, forgive or renounce. Significant life changes may be expected from this lengthy prayer but deeper healing may

---

[17] Definitions and further discussion regarding inner healing, soaking prayer and deliverance may be found in books by Leanne Payne, Mike Flynn and Francis MacNutt referenced in the bibliography.

require multiple sessions. This may also be time for silent "soaking" prayer for support and gradual healing. Give post prayer direction as necessary but always avoid advice-giving.

Getting started and clarifying expectations

If you are just beginning in prayer ministry, you might consider being a silent pray-er and observer with a seasoned prayer team. As you pray alongside the team, you might find you have unspoken insights that other pray-ers later confirm.

Another way to learn and gain confidence is to receive prayer for yourself consistently. Often, the effective words that are prayed over us are the same words we later pray for others as the Holy Spirit brings them to mind.

Lastly, whether we are beginners or experienced prayer team members, we must maintain consistent boundaries and appropriate expectations for prayer situations. That way, much of the anxiety and potential chaos can be avoided for both the pray-er and the pray-ee.

I didn't understand the need for clear expectations until a few years ago. A friend generously offered to pray for me after a late night get-together. I had severe joint pain and I wanted to go to bed. But I also wanted healing. My friend's offer was so kind that I immediately said yes, despite the late hour and my need for sleep.

Unfortunately, in her zeal, my friend did not know when or how to end the prayer time. I expected five-minute "on the street" prayer. She apparently thought it would be lengthy "get-to-the-root-and-get-it-healed" prayer. Not wanting to disappoint her and having horrible boundaries myself, I kept my eyes closed and went along with her well-meaning ministry.

An hour later, prayer was no longer helping. I tried desperately to give "this isn't working and it's time to go to bed" signals but she persisted. I resorted to hoping my husband would notice and gently send her home, which he did...finally. How much easier it would have been for both of us if I had clarified my expectations in advance.

Categories

As we begin to pray for other people, we soon realize just how complex prayer really is. There are so many different ways to pray and so many different needs to pray for. How can we know which direction to go, aside from hearing specific words of knowledge every time?

Knowing some basic categories for prayer can help in our decisions about direction. One or two will probably describe the situation and help bring focus:

- Salvation
- Physical Healing
- Inner or Emotional Healing
- Deliverance
- Healing of the Mind
- Raising the Dead (well, at least this one is obvious!)

Each of these prayer categories has some basic components as well as further implications for how we pray. At the very least, the descriptions can act as a framework to get us started in prayer. For example, if the person needs physical healing, I might expect that I as the pray-er will be praying about, and possibly speaking to, physical symptoms or conditions. On the other hand, if inner healing is indicated, I will be looking for root causes to the current distress or issues requiring forgiveness or confession.

To begin, let's look at each category individually.

Salvation

Praying for someone who wants to know Jesus generally involves a few basic elements but prayer can be phrased in any way that seems appropriate at the time. The individual will need to recognize personal sinfulness or brokenness, confess his or her sins, receive forgiveness, accept Jesus as Savior and Lord, and receive all that the Holy Spirit has to give him or her in order to live this new life in Christ.

Prayer for salvation requires active participation on the part of the person you're praying for. It's not something that he or she receives passively; nor is it something that you can minister apart from the person's involvement. While it is important to help lead the person through the steps (he or she may need to repeat the prayer after you), the person needs to recognize his or her sin, confess it, and invite Jesus into his or her heart. Our role is to help and to encourage, to guide and to bless. Once the person has made a confession, we can pronounce forgiveness (1 John 1:9-10) and lift the burden of sin away. We can pray for the Holy Spirit's power to be released (Acts 1:8).

Physical Healing

A need for physical healing is characterized by a physical pain, condition, deformity, or injury. It may involve a mental or a physical infirmity. There are many possible directions for healing prayer.

Generally, prayer for physical healing involves touch ("laying on of hands") and may involve a spoken word or command, an act of faith, or even deliverance; for example, a deaf and dumb spirit could possibly be a cause of deafness. If the presence of the Lord is especially powerful, the person may sense physical changes or sensations of God's power.

Soaking prayer

One of the most effective but least often used forms of prayer is "soaking prayer." This involves prayer over a lengthy time and is often useful if someone is suffering from a chronic condition, especially one that hasn't responded to more direct short-term prayer. It can be used again and again, even over a period of many weeks or months. In those seasons, we often see healing grow and accumulate over time.

We begin the prayer time by inviting the Holy Spirit to come and minister, praying for God's presence to fill and change the person. We then allow the person simply to rest and sit in the presence of the Lord for an extended time, even an hour or two. Pray-ers who are comfortable with the concept of a "prayer language," a private devotional use of tongues, may find it helpful to pray silently in tongues. Others may want to pray silently over the person with psalms, blessings or words to scriptural worship songs.

Confirmation of healing

Healing must be confirmed by a medical professional. In fact, that is a biblical model. Jesus commanded people to show themselves to the priests, who were the doctors of the day. Medication and psychological or psychiatric treatment are also a means of grace for healing and we never discourage treatment. We also do not recommend that a person should discontinue treatment or delay surgery, etc., even if there is evidence of healing. Again, the person should be advised to go back to his or her doctor for further advice, confirmation, or treatment.

Interconnectedness

Physical and emotional healing are often very interconnected. Physical symptoms and conditions may be linked to underlying emotional wounds. Conversely, emotional symptoms may be a result of physical or hormonal causes, reactions to medicine or their side effects, or chronic pain. It's important to ask the Lord to show us any underlying causes for physical ailments and to deal with any root issues.

Inner or Emotional Healing

Inner healing involves healing of an emotional pain or wound. We must listen both to the person and to the Lord, since emotional healing almost always involves some root issues.

Sometimes our prayers for emotional healing are very direct and focused. For example, the person may need to pray for forgiveness for a sin committed long ago or may need to forgive someone for serious abuse.

In other cases, inner healing may also involve soaking prayer, just as physical healing does. This is especially true if there is no known root to the presenting issue. Soaking prayer may bring relief as the wound or hurt is quietly lifted before the Lord and as He comes and relieves the pain. It may bring to the surface a memory or it may clarify the reason for the emotional pain.

We always lay hands on the person, if he or she is comfortable with that, and we ask the Lord for wisdom in uncovering the root cause. We ask the Lord to remove the pain, minister healing to the wound, and soothe the hurting heart. Self-hatred may need to be renounced. Confession may be in order or the person may need to be forgiven or grant forgiveness.

Very often Jesus will change the person's perspective about the painful incident and that realization may bring significant healing. Other times, the person believes deep lies that Jesus wants to replace or he or she may feel a deep unmet need which we ask Jesus to fill.

On occasion, deliverance is involved either in small or large ways. For example, discouragement might be spiritual rather than emotional; or a demonic spirit could cause undue, excessive and ongoing grieving; or a demon could manifest itself in violent angry outbursts. If the presence of the Lord is especially strong, the person may experience physical sensations of God's power and tangible freedom when an unholy spirit leaves.

Again, as in physical healing, we encourage medication and psychological or psychiatric treatment when necessary. The Lord uses many different ways to bring emotional freedom and we gladly integrate other alternatives if the person wants us to.

Deliverance

Deliverance is needed when one encounters the demonic or a demonized person. To be demonized simply means to be affected by the enemy in a ongoing way. The subject of deliverance really deserves its own book and there are many volumes of material available (both good and bad) on the subject. It is helpful to know a few basics before you begin to pray—there's nothing more unnerving than having a demonic presence take you by surprise! Fortunately, most demonic oppression is taken care of fairly easily. We certainly have no reason to fear the demonic realm, since, "He that is in you is greater than he that is in the world" (1 John 4:4).

In one sense, demonic oppression and demonization are discerned spiritually—we "sense" something is there or we intuit an evil spiritual cause. In other ways, demonization can be "seen"—we suspect it because of what we observe. Symptoms can fall on a wide spectrum and range from imperceptibly minor (e.g., feeling weighed down or having a headache) to obviously major (e.g., having major outbursts of violent anger that the pray-ee cannot remember). It's important to note that not all symptoms are demonic; a headache is usually not caused by a demon. But all demonic oppression is manifested in some symptoms, even if they are almost unnoticed.

We suspect demonic involvement when we see things like persistent patterns that do not respond to other prayer; or unnatural activity (unnatural voice or affect or behavior); or a sense of oppression, sense of bondage, sense of being controlled by a habit or activity, etc.

Deliverance can be as simple as speaking to a condition. For example, I might command a headache to leave if the pain is caused by a spiritual attack. Deliverance can also be major and involve breaking curses, severing generational patterns, or tearing down major demonic strongholds causing paralysis or violent outbursts.

It is not always necessary to know the name of a demon or its reason for being there but it might be helpful. Generally, we don't speak to demons unless they speak to us. Even then, we do not want to be drawn into dialogue with a lying spirit. As one noted prayer minister pointed out, our job is to dialogue with the Lord, not with the enemy. Undue statements directed to the enemy can needlessly stir up a hornet's nest.

When we encounter symptoms that may be demonic, the first thing we pray for is the root cause of the demonization. We want to start by dealing with any underlying condition which may have allowed the enemy to gain a foothold. This can involve receiving or granting forgiveness, or dealing with inner healing issues. On occasion it may be necessary to stop the demonic activity before inner healing may occur, but normally it is the other way around. The stronghold usually stems from an emotional wound, trauma, involvement in witchcraft, a generational pattern or sin, a curse, etc.

Once the root has been dealt with effectively, we can proceed to personal renunciation of any stronghold or demonic influence, repentance, breaking of curses, etc. We have authority to speak to the demon and expel it and we should not be afraid to use that authority.[18] But if the root is left unhealed, the demon may not leave or may come back later.

The demonic manifestation may involve physical actions, even strong ones, so it is natural that expelling a demon may bring physical changes as well. In all cases, be sure to ask the Holy Spirit to fill the space the demon has left so that there is no room for that spirit or its "friends" to return.

Healing of the Mind

This is remarkably similar to inner healing, but involves changing a thought pattern or belief system (Romans 12:2). Healing of the mind may come more easily as a result of prior inner healing. However, it can also be a result of discipleship or the ongoing influence of the Holy Spirit. This is the one healing that often happens without direct prayer.

Praying for a change in belief or thought pattern usually requires healing wounds which underlie the false beliefs. That may involve confession and renunciation of those beliefs, and a purposeful practice of "changing the mind." Healing of the mind also includes cleansing the mind of false or diseased images (especially graphic sexual ones) which the mind has stored. For example, when I am praying for someone who has used pornography, I often pray very authoritatively and actively for the person: "We take these images out of your mind and place them on the cross. We remove the memory of them and wash your mind with the cleansing of Jesus." We can also speak the truth that replaces the false belief if the person we're praying for can appropriate that prayer as more than good advice.

Healing of the mind always involves ongoing submission to the work of the Spirit. He delights to bring truth and freedom to us, and He gives us grace as we learn to cooperate with Him.

---

[18] Luke 10:17-19; Acts 5:12-16; Acts 8:4-8

"Whatever is true, whatever is noble, whatever is right, whatever is pure, whatever is lovely, whatever is admirable—if anything is excellent or praiseworthy—think about such things" (Philippians 4:8).

Raising the Dead

Did you skip to this section to see what you would find? It's not a category we think about very often and we can't interview the dead to find out how to pray.

Praying for resurrection usually involves a spoken word or command, often resulting from a strong surge of faith (or desperation!). It can take many different forms, including speaking life to the person.

Praying for resurrection could also involve all sorts of uncomfortable actions if Scripture is used as a model. Have you lain on top of a dead person lately? Elisha did. I would like to see the dead raised, but I hope this is one model I do not have to use!

End of Life Issues

Ecclesiastes 3 reminds us that there is a season for everything. There is a time appointed for each of us to die. When that time is at hand, it is much more beneficial for the person and their family to receive prayer for end of life issues: care, provision, lack of pain, courage, salvation, peace, comfort for the family, etc.

To continue praying for a miracle, if you are not sure that is the Lord's specific purpose, is cruel and painful for everyone. It does not allow for preparation and comfort. I have seen God clarify when it is the time for death and when it is not. I have prayed, "Lord, is this their time to die?" When we ask the Lord to show us, the prayer team will often sense whether the person will recover or not. Then we take that impression as a word of wisdom from God and pray accordingly.

When Lazarus was ill, Jesus knew that the illness would not ultimately end in death. That is, He knew it was an opportunity for resurrection. He knows the same thing now and He will show us how to pray. We must be very careful to shepherd what God is doing in these instances and not project our desire for a miracle onto a grieving patient or family. After all, our hope is in God, not in healing.

If the person is dying, there are many possible directions for prayer and the Lord will show you which way to go. For example, you might pray for salvation for the one who is dying, if he or she is open and willing; or for relief from pain and anxiety. It would be appropriate to pray for comfort and ease in preparation for the process of dying. If the person knows the Lord there is cause for rejoicing even amid grief and pain. You could pray for the Lord's presence to usher the person into eternity with Him. You—and the family—might release the person finally to be with Jesus. I've seen instances where the person is unconsciously holding onto life for the sake of family members who do not want to let go.

For family and friends, you might pray for comfort, healthy grieving, a peaceful letting-go of their loved one, and hope even during the process. You could pray for grace as they transition back to life without the one who is dying and for provision for their needs. If the person who is dying has been chronically ill the family may have mixed feelings and a degree of guilt about those feelings when the end is finally near.

When it is time for a miracle and for healing, pray boldly for that. If it is not, bring the comfort and care of the Holy Spirit, and His wisdom, to the situation. Your role as a caring "pastor" (the function, not the title) will be much appreciated and is just as valid as praying for God's miraculous intervention. To everything there is a season.

Discovering Root Causes

When people come to us for prayer, they usually come because of their symptoms: pain, disappointment, illness, emotional hurts, fears, etc. It is wise to consider the root causes of those symptoms.

Although it is worth a volume in itself (Aha! The next book in this series!), there are some common roots that underlie many issues:

Sin	Emotional stress	Rejection
Neglect	Abandonment	Abuse
Control	Anger	Unforgiveness
Demonic spirits	Accident	Trauma
Generational patterns	Virus (needs physical healing)	Use of magic /occult

As the roots are dealt with, the symptoms often become less severe, or disappear entirely. At the very least, the symptoms become more manageable; we can begin to establish new behaviors and make healthy choices. The sins that "so easily beset us" no longer control our lives.

General Clarifying Questions

When I am listening to someone describe a need for prayer, dozens of questions are flying through my mind. Many of my questions are conscious. Others are not. Each of the questions and its answer will refine my decisions about how to pray. After determining the setting and the general category for prayer, I may consider the following clarifying questions. You'll undoubtedly add to the list.

- How much time do I have?

- What is the person comfortable with at this time – and for how long?

- What will preserve the person's dignity (place, type of prayer)?

- What is the prominent situation coming to mind here?

- What category or kind of prayer is involved?

- What is the "linchpin" or key area to be healed?

- Might there be a deeper issue than what is being shared?

- Might there be a pattern that the person is not yet aware of?

- If there are many layers, which one is the Holy Spirit addressing now?

- What may be left until later?

- How may I best love this person?

- What is this person able to receive?

- Who is this person comfortable with and able to receive from?

Truth vs. Comfort

Notice that the last two questions (above) focus on the person's possible response to prayer. Although truth might seem to be the highest value when listening and praying, keep in mind that our goal is the healing and freedom of the person. Truly, if the Holy Spirit revealed every truth He knows about us all at once it would crush us. He waits for the right time and so must we. A better question than "What is the truth?" might be, "What will allow this person to agree and move forward?" or "What will best minister to him or her?" or "What will minister hope and life?"

And, as we shall see next, "What will meet *their* need, not mine?"

Motives – Theirs and Ours

Too often, we as pray-ers are not aware of our own motives, which can create great discomfort for the person receiving prayer. It can also hinder the work of the Holy Spirit.

For example, imagine that I need prayer for physical healing and you begin to pray for me. You sense my pain and want me to be healed. However, if your desire becomes an overriding need, I may sense that need and begin to respond to it. I might notice some subtle physical changes and say that I have been healed — even if I have not been healed. Why? Not because I am trying to be dishonest. Rather, I am trying to make you, the pray-*er*, feel more comfortable. I am trying to encourage *you*. I feel your intense desire and respond to it. It's backward but it's common.

Instead, we as pray-*ers* should be the ones to create safety so those who receive prayer can be honest. We must know our own hearts and motives so that we do not project our needs and desires onto the ones we're praying for. Otherwise, they may unconsciously, or even consciously, stop responding to the Lord and start responding to *us*. The person needing prayer should not feel pressure to reassure the pray-er.

How do we know our own hearts? Here are some questions to ask as we prepare to pray for others:

- Do I need to speak out what I hear, regardless of whether it may be better to remain silent?
- Do I need to tell the truth without regard for whether the person is ready to hear it?
- Do I need to sound good?
- Do I need to "succeed" in prayer?
- Do I need to sound knowledgable or profound?
- Do I need to solve the problem and fix the person?

- Do I need to "defend" God's desire to heal or to ensure that healing happens?
- Do I need to be nice or be perceived as nice?
- Do I need to be affirmed as prophetic?

If you are struggling with several of these needs, don't worry; you're not alone. It may be a good idea to ask a trusted friend or prayer team member to pray with you before you pray for someone else. You don't need to be "totally fixed" in order to pray for another person but it certainly helps to know your own issues and inclinations. That way you can guard against your tendencies and give them to the Lord so that He can begin to heal you as well.

Remember, prayer ministry is not about you. That should be a relief! It's about the person you're praying for. As a pray-er, it's your responsibility to value the person you're praying for more than your own need to hear and do things correctly, and more than your need to see the problem fixed.

Having said all this, it still may be difficult to know how to begin. There are no formulas, no easy 1-2-3 answers; you still have to listen and then R-I-S-K. But there are some structures that will help.

Chapter Seventeen
Interview Prayer Model

The "Interview Prayer" is one good way to start when praying for others. As time goes on, you'll be free to discard the exact steps and develop your own style of praying. Until then, it provides a comfortable template to fall back on (see a two-page summary of this template in the appendix). As always, listen to the Lord for specific direction. If He shows you something specific to do, abandon the model and just do what He shows you.

Before prayer

Before prayer, it is essential that everyone—you, the team, and the person you're praying for—knows the boundaries and guidelines that will make prayer safe. Confidentiality and refraining from giving advice are the primary requirements for the team; honesty and sharing personally are the goals for the recipient. If the person requesting prayer does not feel safe, very little can be accomplished.

1. Interview

Interview the person: "Where does it hurt?" Listen both to the person and to God. You only need to know the basics of the person's problem. Don't try to provide a rational answer or give advice. Keep the interview brief.

Understand the length of time you have available. The goal is to get enough information to begin to pray, not to talk or counsel. You don't need a word of knowledge if you can just ask the person what the problem is. Jesus received words of knowledge but he also asked questions. He wanted to focus precisely on target:

> When the spirit saw Jesus, it immediately threw the boy into a convulsion. He fell to the ground and rolled around, foaming at the mouth. Jesus asked the boy's father, "How long has he been like this?" "From childhood," he answered. (Mark 9:21-22)

> They called to the blind man, "Cheer up! On your feet! He's calling you." Throwing his cloak aside, he jumped to his feet and came to Jesus. "What do you want me to do for you?" Jesus asked him. The blind man said, "Rabbi, I want to see." "Go," said Jesus, "your faith has healed you." Immediately he received his sight and followed Jesus along the road. (Mark 10:51-52)

Asking what the person wants is essential and the best place to start; we should always pray for their perceived need. However, sometimes we find people who really don't want to be healed or whose healing need is not what is obviously "wrong." In those cases, we are wise to ask more questions before we pray.

Gathering information

What do you do when a person shares a prayer need or a problem but he or she doesn't understand the roots? Which questions might you ask?

There are many possible interview questions but a long list can be overwhelming. Instead, it's important to draw the person into *brief* conversation to find out what you need to know.

Making dozens of queries in a pointed fashion is not only intimidating, it might make the person feel like a prisoner being interrogated.

Having said that, here's the long list:

- How long has this been going on?
- What else happened around the same time that it started? What else was going on in your life then?
- Were there any major crises or traumas around that time as well? (Job change, betrayal, death in family, divorce, abuse, financial stress, etc.)
- Does this remind you of other times in your life, especially earlier times? Does it go back further than the present?
- Have you felt this way in the past, especially as a child? Is this a pattern?
- Have you received prayer about this before? If so, what changed as a result?
- Is there a medical diagnosis? This can be good or bad — good if it defines the struggle, or bad if it becomes a "curse."

If you are praying during a lengthy scheduled prayer appointment you may want to consider using a confidential questionnaire. If possible, ask the person requesting prayer to fill it out before the appointment, when he or she has time to think about personal history. Review the form before the prayer appointment, if only for a few minutes, and pray for wisdom and discernment. The questionnaire provides valuable background information, such as spiritual background, occult / witchcraft history, New Age practices (Reiki, etc.), secret society involvement (Masonic lodge, etc.), medical history, prescriptions used, etc. It also saves time in the prayer appointment and can help you to spot potential patterns or areas of need. Not surprisingly, most counseling ministries do this routinely. If you're doing in-depth prayer ministry, you need to know someone's in-depth spiritual background.

2. Make a diagnostic decision. Why is the problem there? What are the roots?

Why does the person have the problem? Look for physical, emotional, spiritual, generational, and sinful patterns or roots. Especially look for the roots of issues, not just the symptoms. Be aware that many times people focus on their sinful behaviors, which may mask the deeper underlying needs or root causes.

This is the time to make a tentative decision about why the problem is there and how to pray. It will inform not only the direction for prayer but also the kind of prayers that help.

3. What kind of prayer will help?

What kind of prayer will be most effective? Look back at the categories in the previous chapter to delineate what comes next. Use your diagnosis (above) to help you choose the direction for prayer. Does the person need emotional healing? Deliverance? Salvation? Is the appropriate prayer one of intercession? Command? Deliverance? Confession and forgiveness? You may not know *exactly* how to proceed at this point but you will know *something*. Start there. Then listen for further direction as you begin to pray.

4. Pray

Lay hands on the person
Why? Scripture tells us to lay hands on the sick for healing— Jesus did it. There is healing in touch. That's one way Jesus healed and blessed people:

Jesus had compassion on them and touched their eyes. Immediately they received their sight and followed him. (Matthew 20:34)

Then little children were brought to Jesus for him to place his hands on them and pray for them. But the disciples rebuked those who brought them. Jesus said, "Let the little children come to me, and do not hinder them, for the kingdom of heaven belongs to such as these." When he had placed his hands on them, he went on from there. (Matthew 19:13-15)

Where? Where it hurts is good—within modest boundaries, of course. Laying hands on a person's shoulder, back or head (without mussing hair) are usually acceptable and safe.

Always ask permission first. For some people touch symbolizes abuse instead of blessing. This is particularly an issue for women who have suffered abuse from men. In some cases, just having a man's touch—or even his presence—can cause an abuse victim to shut down anything that the Lord might want to do. Of course, this can happen with men as well; but a majority of cases such as this involve women. Always ask whether the person you're praying for is comfortable with "laying on of hands." If he or she is not, don't push. The Holy Spirit can still work. "May we lay hands on you when we pray?" is always a good question.

One obvious caveat: Don't put your hands anywhere you're not supposed to touch. Be aware of the person's dignity and be sensitive to personal boundaries and space.

Fortunately, most people receiving prayer are gracious, but it's easy to find yourself in an embarrassing situation. I remember standing behind a woman while I was praying for her. When I reached around to hug her after finishing prayer, she suddenly turned at the same instant and I unintentionally hugged...her chest. I was enormously embarrassed! I don't think she was uncomfortable, but I certainly was. It's always wise to be careful with personal touch.

Invite the Holy Spirit to come

"Wherever two or three are gathered" we know Jesus is already present by the Holy Spirit. However, we always desire an increased sense of the Spirit's presence, both for comfort and healing, and we need His leading so we know *what* to pray. The Holy Spirit's increased tangible presence helps us focus on Jesus and on what He is saying or doing.

When you invite the Holy Spirit's presence expect that He will come. It's best to encourage the person you are praying for simply to be receptive. It's hard to talk and receive at the same time—and prayer is a form of talking. You can encourage the person by suggesting that he or she relax and focus on the Lord: "Don't pray, just relax. Be patient, close your eyes, and focus on Jesus." Then just say, "Come Holy Spirit" and wait. No hype or theatrics are needed.

Ask God What He Wants To Do,
Listen to What He Says, and Do it or Pursue it

Do it: Do what God says. Command. Rebuke. Intercede. Speak to conditions. Minister to the heart. Do whatever it is you see or hear.

Or Pursue it: Interact with the person receiving prayer; look for what God is doing or watch how the pray-ee is responding. It's common for you or the person you're praying for to see a picture in which Jesus is doing something. If so, simply describe what you see..."I see Jesus and He's ..." If necessary, ask the person if the picture makes sense in their situation. Note that we don't *suggest* a picture or scenario unless Jesus reveals one; we do, however, pursue any image that He gives us.

Watch: After listening to the Lord, open your eyes when you pray. You may see physical reactions or responses to what is going on. Or you may see clues that your prayer is not being received or even that you are heading in the wrong direction. That's important information.

If you're receiving prayer, *please* **close your eyes.** As a prayer minister, I find it incredibly unnerving when the person receiving prayer suddenly opens his or her eyes and stares at me. More than once I've had to shut my eyes quickly. And tightly. Mostly it was because staring at the wide-eyed pray-ee was too difficult, uncomfortable, and distracting. In addition, I did not want to make the person feel any more uncomfortable than he or she already was. After all, if the person was incredibly engaged with the Lord and very comfortable with intimacy and prayer, he or she probably wouldn't have opened his or her eyes to begin with.

Check in: Ask the person what's going on if you don't know—and continue to ask. What does the person "see" Jesus doing? What is he or she feeling? What is occurring to him or her as you pray? Certainly, if you do not know what is going on, ask the person and continue to ask periodically until it's clear. Beware of getting into lengthy conversation at this point since your focus is prayer but you can always "check in."

Watching and asking questions are more than just good etiquette. Either practice can keep your prayers from getting seriously off-track. One day, many years ago, I followed my usual pattern and went forward for prayer after church. I did not know exactly what God was doing but I could definitely pinpoint at least two things I needed: I wanted someone to encourage me in prayer and I wanted help discerning the path through some lurking issues.

A prayer team member approached me and, without asking, laid hands firmly on my head. Fine, I thought; he hears something and wants to impart it. I knew him to be a prophetic type, a trusted prayer minister with a proven track record. I expected that he would hear from God.

That day, however, he was wrong. Pushing firmly on my forehead, he loudly proclaimed a "missionary anointing" over my life. Again, and again, and again. Startled, I recoiled and frowned but I didn't open my eyes. That was completely *not* what God was doing. I wanted prayer for a personal issue, not for an anointing I was not seeking and felt no leading toward. Of course, if God wanted it... I hesitated a moment, wondering. But deep inside, I knew his prayer wasn't right.

I thought surely this zealous pray-er would see me back up and turn my head away. He continued for what seemed like forever. I winced, backed up further, and finally just gave up. I stood there, completely unengaged, until he finished. Then I ran back to my seat as fast as I could.

As far as I can tell, this well-intentioned prayer minister never looked up, never checked to see if I was uncomfortable, never asked whether I resonated with his "word," and never questioned the timing or applicability of his prayer. I don't think he ever realized that I was not receiving his prophetic declaration. If only he had "checked in" with me during prayer, I might have been more receptive and we might have discovered some real underlying issues.

Although it would have helped in that case, checking in as you pray is not really designed to keep you from praying the wrong things. Instead, it helps clarify what the person is responding to and it can reap huge benefits with very little effort.

> Some people brought a blind man and begged Jesus to touch him. He took the blind man by the hand and led him outside the village. When he had spit on the man's eyes and put his hands on him, Jesus asked, "Do you see anything?" He looked up and said, "I see people; they look like trees walking

around." Once more Jesus put his hands on the man's eyes. Then his eyes were opened, his sight was restored, and he saw everything clearly. (Mark 8.22)

In this Scripture, either Jesus didn't know if the man was healed or he wanted more information. When the man described only partial healing, Jesus prayed a second time, and the man saw! After the second prayer, the healing was complete.

Two points to notice about what Jesus did: first, He asked questions after He prayed. Second, He prayed twice. If *Jesus* prayed a second time surely we can pray more times than that. This is one reason we never feel awkward praying for the same condition as many times as needed.

Maintain the right balance of involvement: Keep the person involved—but not too involved. There is a fine line between the two. On one hand, it is far better to have the person vitally engaged than completely passive. For example, if a person has sinned he or she may need to speak out a confession. Or if the person was involved in inappropriate relationships, he or she may need to renounce those attachments, out loud, in prayer. Too often people receiving prayer want to have healing "dropped" on them, as if they have no part to play.

On the other hand, many people simply try too hard; they continue to pray or participate (talk) so much that it's impossible for them to receive. Remember, receiving from God requires relaxation and receptivity. Whether the people we pray for are listening for what He's saying or sensing His presence, they need to perceive quietly what the Lord is doing in order to receive it. If they actively talk and pray too much it's impossible for them to be quiet and focus on Jesus.

Interact with others on the team. If you need to, ask another team member what's going on during prayer. When Phil and I pray for people, I can always tell when Phil is hearing something from the Lord. (Did I mention that Phil rolls his eyes when he hears a word from God?) I catch his glance and say, "Do you have something Phil?" Then, of course, he feels obligated, err…encouraged to say something, which is precisely what I am hoping he will do (of course I'm joking, but yes, I routinely repent for manipulation). You may need to communicate with other team members with your eyes. If you need to concentrate, close your eyes to focus on Jesus.

Does the person know Jesus? If you haven't asked in the interview phase and if you have any doubt, ask gently whether the person knows Jesus. Often God will use healing for evangelism. Receiving the Lord can be the greatest healing of all.

Use the active voice to minister: When you have an indication of what to pray or if you see or hear something from the Lord, here are some ways to minister the picture, image, or word:

- Tell the person the picture and ask what he or she thinks it means.

- Pray the intent of the picture using the active voice where possible.

  For example, if you see a flowing waterfall you might say, "I bless you with the flowing water of God, running down over you" or "I see a picture of a waterfall and I think the Lord is _____ ."

- Command the condition you're praying for to be healed.

- Declare the picture to be true and come into being.

- Warfare: If you see Jesus warring against something, ask the Lord if you have permission to DO what you see. The answer will often be yes. If so, stand against the attack of the enemy (not Satan, but his minions. Satan is probably nowhere around – he has bigger things to do).

- Intercede (only if you have no other choice, or are strongly led to).

When to stop praying:

When the situation warrants it. If the situation becomes unduly emotional, loud, or difficult, and you are in a public setting, it's probably best to quiet the person, stop praying, and find someone to sit with him or her. Any in-depth prayer may be handled by another team or a referral at a later time. At the very least, quiet the situation and calmly walk with the person to another room. The person is probably as disturbed by the situation as you are and he or she will value the privacy.

If you are in an in-depth prayer appointment and the situation becomes more than you can handle, quiet the situation and refer the pray-ee to another team or a supervisor.

When it's over or you are out of time. In most situations, prayer has a natural ending point. Either there is nothing else to pray or the session seems to be finished. But whether or not you think the prayer time is finished, if the person says it's over then it's over. If you hear from God that your work is done then it's over. If you are out of time…then it's over. And if you simply cannot think of anything else to pray look around at the team. If they can't think of anything to pray either then it's over.

We often overlook the obvious when we come to the end of prayer. If there's no progress it's fine to stop. There's no need to prolong the session.

I have been in many situations in which I thought there was more to pray but the person I was praying for opened his or her eyes and said "Amen." Conversely, I have received prayer many times when I knew the prayer time was complete but the pray-ers kept praying. No one knew when to end. I waited, hoping someone had something to add and waited (for an interminably L-O-N-G time), until finally someone tentatively ventured a feeble "Amen?"

The easiest way to handle endings is to look around. Is the person still "receiving" and connecting with God, enjoying His presence? Is anyone on the team still hearing words from God that need to be prayed? Make eye contact with each person on the team, if you can, and end when it seems appropriate to everyone involved.

How to stop praying: Bless the person and ask God to seal what He's has done. The Holy Spirit has been present throughout the prayer session, but we want Him to protect and continue the process as the person goes home. Bless the pray-ee with His continued presence and ask the Holy Spirit to seal the work He's done. Pray for the protection of the Holy Spirit over the person and say amen.

5. Post-prayer

Is there anything the person needs to do to continue? If necessary, help him or her to make decisions and plans for next steps but don't lapse into counseling. This is time for the person to enjoy (or recover from) what God has done and for everyone to rest.

Healing can be a difficult process if pain surfaces in the moment, which it often does. There may be tears and suffering but they should give way to joy, peace, and comfort by the end.

After the person goes home—time for the team: It may be helpful to de-process with the team. It also may be helpful to pray a "cleansing prayer" over the team, spiritually washing off anything that might have subtly or not so subtly affected their minds, hearts, emotions, or spirits. Demonic spirits that have been expelled might leave "slime" or try to attack the team but they are easily taken care of by praying after the session.

Emotionally wrenching trauma may have been revealed and may be especially difficult for sensitive team members. You do not want team members to retain the weight of what they have heard. Ask the Lord to wash and cleanse; pray for His protection, His joy, and His peace over the team. Remind them that what they have heard, seen, and done is confidential. Then go home and rest.

Chapter Eighteen
Processing After Prayer

Sometimes, after a prayer appointment, I am left with even more questions than when I started. "What happened there?" "Do we need to follow-up?" "How effective was it really?" "How can I help this person further?" "What do I do with what was shared?" "Do I have any further responsibility?" "Was it my fault that the person wasn't healed?" *and the worst one:* "I know if someone else had prayed, it would have been better."

Most of these questions deserve much thought and consideration. Some have straightforward answers. But other times, immediately after prayer we are hit with an onslaught of reactions, feelings, and questions simply because the enemy loves to attack us because of the work the Lord and we accomplished. The accuser's questions are best given to Jesus and ignored. Prayers of protection and cleansing are helpful, and so is rest; prayer ministry is exhausting.

What do I do with the difficult memories that were shared?

In prayer ministry we often hear memories, words and confessions that we wish we hadn't heard. (My bad memory can actually be an asset!) The more people we pray for, the fewer specifics we can remember, but some cases remain that are genuinely difficult to hear and even harder to forget. How do we respond?

Respond as Jesus did, with compassion and mercy. He expressed compassion and mercy to everyone in pain and to every repentant sinner. To the woman caught in adultery, Jesus said, "Let him who is without sin throw the first stone" (John 8:3-11). When a sinful woman poured perfume over Jesus' feet, the Pharisees and disciples thought He would "know what kind of woman she was," but instead He blessed her for blessing Him (Luke 7:36-50). *Nowhere* does Jesus condemn anyone who is sinful, except those who try to hide it. The Pharisees, who thought they had no sin and hid their hypocrisy, were often the objects of his scorn. He *really* exposed their sin and had some rather strong words to say about them.

Intercede. Jesus did not act on everything He knew, but often chose to wait (recall our discussion of "what do I do with what I see and hear from the Lord"). Similarly, we are often called to intercede and wait for the Lord to act or to soften hearts.

Keep in mind the psychological perspective. Why did the person ask for prayer? Most people come with some level of guilt and shame and a desire to stop the problem or regain control. They've tried and failed or they wouldn't be asking for help. Or the Holy Spirit may be convicting or prompting them. Imagine yourself in their place and understand their motivation and desperation. Be merciful and expect the Holy Spirit to complete the work He has begun.

Be unshockable. There is nothing new under the sun; Jesus is not surprised by the person's actions or situation. He does not shame the person, ever, and neither should we. We are all sinners and capable of far worse than anything we have heard from anyone else. When I realize my own vulnerability to sin and think of what I might do in a similar situation, I suddenly find myself judging far less and extending more compassion. "Judge not lest you be judged" is not a comfortable Scripture but it surely is true.

If, during the prayer time you do not know what to do or you need help, don't show your shock, dismay or fear. "Dial down" or close the prayer time gently and refer the person to someone more experienced. You may say something like, "You know, there's someone else who has a lot of experience in this area and would be a real help to you; would you mind if I ask her to join us?"

If the person does not want you to refer him or her to someone else, then you must not. However, you do not need to continue on with more prayer times.

If you need help and advice from a supervisor or from someone with more experience, make a point to find it. We've all run into roadblocks in prayer at one time or another. However, as you ask for advice, remember confidentiality; don't refer to names or identifiable situations without permission.

Continue to fast and pray for the person if it seems appropriate. If the person has scheduled another prayer appointment with you or if ministry will continue for some time, it may be helpful to keep interceding; fasting may enable breakthrough. The Holy Spirit will lead you in this; He wants the person healed and set free more than you do.

What am I responsible for?

After prayer, it helps to remember that you are not responsible *for* very much at all. You are responsible *to* provide a safe environment and to listen to the person and the Lord. You are responsible to love and care for the person and to preserve his or her dignity. But you are not responsible *for* them.

When you pray, your job is facilitator, pray-er, listener, and intercessor. The most important interaction is between the person and Jesus, not between the person and you. You are there to take the person to Jesus, to do what He shows you to do, to observe, and to assist. For example, where there is sin or pain, help lift it off the person and take it to Jesus (or to the image of the cross, if that is more useful). Smooth the way between Jesus and the person. He is the one who will empower the healing, not you.

How refreshing it is to realize how much we are *not* responsible for. We are *not* responsible for the person's action, reaction, repentance, behavior, or attitude. We are *not* responsible for the results of the prayer time or whether the person is healed. We are *not* responsible to "keep sin out of the camp." That is the job of the Spirit and He does it well and gently, according to the person's ability to repent or receive His work. (Besides, if we're getting rid of sin and sinners… you and I are in big trouble, too.)

Beware of the temptation to control—during prayer or after.

It's very easy to be captured by the intense desire to see people healed or to help them change. It's tempting to try to keep them from harm or to impact what they do. However, these desires can easily lapse into control and control is not ours to take, especially in prayer.

Control, or the lack of it, is a major challenge as we pray. What is control? Control is either *forcing* something to happen or forcibly *preventing* something from happening; it is one of the "MUST NOTS" of prayer ministry.

The Holy Spirit must be in control, not us. If people fail or fall after we pray we gladly lift them up and help them. If appropriate, and if requested, we may exhort or teach, but we must not attempt to control their actions, reactions or behavior. Jesus always leaves room for free will, and so must we.

What if they aren't healed?

What do we do when the people we pray for aren't healed? The short answer is that we keep praying unless the Lord changes our direction. As much as we would like it to, healing does not always happen. We don't know why. Theologians have debated this for centuries; we will certainly not resolve that debate here, but at least we can agree on a few points.

It is *not ever* the person's "fault" if he or she is not healed. It is not necessarily because of his or her "lack of faith," and we never (ever) allow people to believe that a change in attitude is all that is needed for them to be healed. This thinking only leaves them under a huge burden. Like hamsters on a wheel, they are left to work endlessly at something they cannot control and can never accomplish: their own healing. We never want people receiving prayer to leave with heavier hearts than when they came.

Yes, faith is always present when healing happens, but we never know whose faith is responsible. In Scripture, sometimes it is the person's faith. Sometimes it is a friends' faith. Sometimes it is someone else's faith, and sometimes it is the Lord's. So we pray, encourage those who need healing, and leave the results to God. And we always continue to intercede.

It is clear in Scripture that not everyone was healed all the time. Sometimes "the power of the Lord was present for Him to heal the sick" (Luke 5:17). By implication then, sometimes it wasn't. Sometimes he healed them all. Other times we only hear about one. In Mark 5, Jesus walked through the crowd and only noticed that *one* woman who had been bleeding for twelve years had touched him. By implication, others were not so affected. Why? We don't know. But we do know that we can trust Jesus to do what is right, at the right time.

We also know that sickness and disease are a result of the Fall and are not part of the Kingdom of God. But, as we discussed earlier, the Kingdom is not yet fully here. Sometimes we see healing. Other times we don't. God does not inflict sickness as judgment, though He may allow it for a reason, to make a point, as He did with Job. He always acts and He always cares—and He always desires to change our lives. Our job is to find out specifically what He is doing and focus on that. Along the way, we pray for healing and we pray for miracles. We rejoice in what He does and we keep praying until He either heals or tells us to stop.

Post-Prayer attack: prayers for protection

The period after prayer is a prime time for the enemy to discourage or attack the Lord's warriors (that would be us!). As we mentioned in post-prayer guidelines, it may be helpful to pray with the team after the prayer time is over and the pray-ee has left. We don't want to take home anything left behind after prayer, either spiritual or emotional debris, and we want to be protected as we continue with life and ministry.

We need to be on guard and to pray for protection. However, the form of the prayers does not matter. Both John and Paul remind us that it is the Spirit who guides us into all truth and He will tell us what we need to pray, and when:

> But the Counselor, the Holy Spirit, whom the Father will send in my name, will teach you all things and will remind you of everything I have said to you. (John 14:26)

> We do not know what we ought to pray for, but the Spirit himself intercedes for us with groans that words cannot express. (Romans, 8:26)

It isn't essential to use specific formulaic prayers in everyday situations, unless you find you are susceptible to mood changes or to "picking up" the infirmities or pain or inclinations of the people you're praying for. If you are consistently not doing well try using specific prayers for protection or cleansing and see what happens. As examples, helpful prayers from Francis and Judith MacNutt and Mike Flynn are included in the Appendix.

These prayers may be helpful tools in your tool belt, but they should not be used in a superstitious or legalistic way. Prayers, after all, are not formulas but relational conversations.

Francis MacNutt, author of many classic works on healing prayer, maintains that sometimes it is helpful to use the words of specifically crafted prayers. He notes that these particular words are the same elements found in the "prayers" and curses of Satanism and witchcraft. Certainly we wish to counter specifically those curses and at times we need the help of very precise prayers; however, in most cases we can simply pray for general concepts that we know to be true: we want to be *protected, washed clean, and freed from all effects* of the enemy.

What does the person do next to continue on?

All of us need support and prayer, whether for specific healing issues or for surviving and overcoming in daily life. Sometimes people need to try various avenues on their way to healing— further inner healing appointments, deliverance, counseling, teaching, medical help, psychological help, or recovery groups. But for many people, a support group, whether ongoing or short-term, can provide the consistent care and prayer they need in a healthy environment.

We find safety in small groups. We receive and give and we learn how to pray in those groups. With that support and prayer, we can all grow together into the ministering body of Christ. But we need safe prayer ministers who bring hope and healing to the wounded. We need caregivers who are willing to love even when it's messy. We need pastors who will listen. We need prophets who can speak the comfort of the Lord and help hold up the arms of those who are weak. Most of all, we need leaders who are unshockable and who will not shame, fix, judge, or blame.

Our next challenge is to find and develop those leaders who will provide safe places and small groups where healing may continue. Are you one of those leaders? Are you willing? Will you let God move through you? Will you give it a try?

Chapter Nineteen
Small Support Groups for Prayer

Ask me how to learn anything about prayer ministry and I'll tell you the same thing: practice in small groups. Whether you want to receive prayer or give it, small groups are a linchpin in the healing prayer journey.

Well-led praying support groups are some of the healthiest places around. They're small, they're safe, they're private. They offer plenty of room to grow and learn and lots of grace to cover mistakes.

But they have to be safe. By safe I don't mean a group which claims to love but has a thinly-disguised agenda of prophetic truth-telling and advice and a determination to "fix" every problem with exhortation. Nor do I mean a saccharine acceptance of all things sinful in the name of compassion. Rather, I mean a group with redemptive grace in its DNA. A group where the members know in their bones that "there but for the grace of God go I." They know the power of God to bring people back home to the healing freedom of Jesus. That makes a group safe.

How do we find such good leaders and groups? How do we instill this DNA? Given that Jesus often compared us to sheep, please permit me a real-life example. When we first toured the highlands of Scotland twenty-five years ago, we stayed at an intriguing B&B, a working sheep farm. Our host, the aging sheep farmer, gloated over his intelligent sheep dogs, all collies. When we asked how he found such amazing dogs, he chuckled at our naiveté: "Ya breed 'em fer ther brains."

So it is with small groups; we start them and breed them with this DNA. The healthiness, the safety and grace, the longing to hear just what God is doing and do only that, the love for prayer, and the passion for freedom must all be bred into their genes. To be more specific, those qualities must be inculcated in their leaders' genes.

An Example

The room was crowded. Stuffed, actually. There were people on couches. People on chairs. People on the floor. People by the table. People *under* the table (literally). People of all ages, with all manner of traumas, struggles, and dysfunctions. Happy people, sad people, laughing people, mad people, and even one in the bedroom crying as she remembered abuse. We were a motley crew, at best. Who would ever have put all those people with all those dysfunctions in one room?

Some struggled with past abuse, some with fear and anxiety, some with gender issues, one with paranoid schizophrenia, and another two with dissociative identity disorder. One couldn't forget her abuse and another didn't want to remember. One was a perpetrator in his distant past, and another had vague memories of strange rituals with candles. Several fought with addictions to pornography and many others wrestled with codependency. And along the way, we all coped with more "normal" life struggles: new babies, rigorous academic demands, surgeries, engagements, marriages, and jobs.

We had only one common denominator and it was what held us together for the several years that we met: we were all completely desperate for Jesus. Without Him, every one of us knew we'd be incapacitated, lost, in the hospital, addicted, divorced, drunk, or dead.

We had found a place to hold onto Jesus together, a safe place to cry and to share, a place to pray and to receive from God. We could worship and learn and hold each other up.

Did I mention we could pray?

It was an amazing place to pray and to listen. Almost every week, someone would say the same thing: "But I've *never* heard from the Lord except *here*! I *never* see pictures like this."

Those "nevers" didn't last long. Our desperation led us to listen hard and to pray boldly. Never before, or since, have I seen a group like it. Somehow, whether despite or because of our brokenness, we came together into a community cherished and valued by the Lord and He blessed us immeasurably. We saw more visions, miracles, faith, healing, change, and hope in that room than we could ever imagine. We *needed* Jesus and He came through.

How did it happen? How did God bring this wonderful yet broken group together and bless us so deeply? Much of the answer is *mystery*: sometimes "it" just happens; "God" just happens. He shows up and answers the cries of hurting hearts.

But some of what drew us together was purposefully planned and it can be learned.

Where do we start?

We start with good leaders, who are willing to be vulnerable, transparent and open, leaders who are willing to face the problems in their lives and deal with them honestly. These are leaders who are not interested in themselves and not overly concerned with how much they know or how much the group must learn. They are like good collies for their small group sheep, listening for the whistle of the shepherd and knowing the boundaries of the field.

Vulnerable small groups and their leaders put up with a lot of brokenness, but they also recognize that the Holy Spirit will not leave people there. Supportive small groups provide a place to receive and to recover hope in relationship with God. They encourage all of us to give love, relationship, hope, and prayer, even when we'd rather not do so.

And strangely, as we give we find our own needs met. We are changed not only through receiving prayer but by praying for others. How often God does in us exactly what we have just prayed for someone else! The act of giving is often psychologically safer than receiving; as we pray for others the Lord uses that door to slip in, un-noticed, and minister to our needs, changing our lives.

As we meet every week to worship, care, share, and pray, the small group becomes a microcosm of the church, a place to be honest and to admit our weaknesses, and a place for grace. We can reach out with love because there is no longer shame in being human and being real. As we give grace to one another, the group becomes the most natural place in the world to invite our friends, and they, too, can receive hope and healing as God "shows up" in their midst.

Where do we go from here?

Our small aim is to allow every group member to encounter God, to learn to listen and pray, to feel supported and loved, to share (briefly), and to receive prayer—every week.

However, we have a larger ambition: our Big Hairy Audacious Goal (BHAG, in business parlance) is to be so in tune with God, listening and doing what He is doing, that we see God radically "show up" and heal and change all of our lives—every week. We want every person to feel so safe, loved, and changed by God that they can't wait to "go and tell;" to bring the world to see what God has done and to be changed and loved as well.

Isn't that the way it happened in the early church? God was at work. Everyone knew it. Everyone participated. Everyone prayed. They lived in community. God was among them. All their needs were met and the world came to watch, join in, and go out to spread the Good News.

That's what we want. Renewal. Revival. Change. Healing. We want to affect and infect the world. This happens in relationship and prayer, in communities that share, one life at a time.

Chapter Twenty
The Kingdom of God on the Street... or the Mission Field

We love our small groups.

We love seeing people set free through emotional healing.

We love listening to God and doing what He's doing.

But small groups, inner healing prayer, and listening prayer have largely been activities contained within the church. Instead, being a stealth agent of the Kingdom of God and "praying what you hear" necessitate missionary thinking. Can you imagine what listening—and praying with authority— would do on the street? And in the world?

Jesus knew that signs and wonders were meant to be a witness to the world. He knew these acts demonstrated God's Kingdom and convinced onlookers that His message was real. Miracles opened the doors of skeptical hearts. That's what happened again and again in the New Testament. People followed Jesus because they *saw*, were changed, and believed. How many people? Five thousand after Pentecost. Cornelius's family and friends. Beggars. Lepers. The wounded and lame. They came by ones or by households or by hundreds, but they came.

Jesus didn't ask someone to believe first then receive healing. Instead, He acted. He had compassion and He demonstrated His love. The task of growing the Kingdom always seemed to include *doing* something, a real demonstration of power accompanying His words.

Clearly, this Kingdom message wasn't meant to be restricted to a small conclave of believers. It broke into the society with the force of a tornado, shattering assumptions, worldviews, and theologies.

It changed the world then. Could it change the world now? Could it change the world *I* live in?

Struggling to make sense of this in my early years of ministry, I once asked our pastor how to do healing prayer for people who don't know Jesus, in the workplace or in the mall. How would he do it? "The same way you do it here," he answered. "Well, for how long? I mean, what do you *say*? How long does it *take*?" I queried, wondering exactly how weird this was going to be. "Oh, it takes about seven seconds. I ask the Holy Spirit to come, listen quickly, speak to the condition, and say amen. Then I leave. That's it."

I cringed. Uh-huh. Right. On the street. Yup.

Outside the church walls was not a safe place for me. I was not raised in the church, but I matured there. Like a cultivated flower in a rarified hot-house climate, I learned about the gifts of the Holy Spirit, listening, healing, and God's presence in conferences, Sunday services, Wednesday night prayer meetings and Monday night small groups. Yet, the rest of my life didn't connect with my church life.

Now I was confronted with the clear message that the Kingdom was meant for the streets. This was a revolutionary thought.

But why not? Isn't this what Jesus did? He didn't hide in someone's house and lock the door. Yes, he did ban loud mourners when he spoke to the little girl who had died and she woke up—but usually he was out in public.

Somehow this revelation was not reassuring.

It meant that I had to do something with what I was learning. I had to venture beyond my safe, comfortable little groups. I had to watch for God's agenda in my everyday world, at the store, on the job, at the beach, or on the internet.

I could no longer ignore my neighbor's broken ankle, telling her I hoped she felt better. I had to offer to pray. I couldn't be quiet when a waitress showed me her wrist brace and told me that carpel tunnel syndrome kept her from doing her job. I had to offer to pray. When a friend mentioned her cousin who had been in a vegetative state for years, four of us found ourselves in a hospital room, trying to listen to God and do what we heard.

None of those opportunities resulted in miracles, nor did they launch a healing revival, but they were certainly good practice.

After our first tentative steps outside the church walls, Phil and I were hungry for more. We wanted to see God act in bigger ways in a bigger world. But we were not prepared for what happened.

Healing changes people

Susan was a student I'd worked with several years before. She had heard our stories about healing; she'd even been involved in some of our stories. When she visited us just before her wedding, I didn't expect that it would test our intentions to go into the world to pray.

Susan's younger sister had just finished her first year of college when she discovered her illness. Arriving home after the last week of the semester, she landed in the doctor's office for blood tests. Several days later, Susan and her family were stunned by the results: acute hepatitis (officially Hepatitis Non A and Non B stemming from mononucleosis). With no time before the wedding, it looked like one very important member of the wedding party would be missing.

Susan wasn't sure what it meant yet, although she knew it didn't look good. Her mother, however, was devastated. She showed up at our door, distraught over her younger daughter's illness and her older one's disrupted wedding plans. To her, this was becoming a major disaster.

Talking with Susan's mom, I thought about praying, but I hesitated. Susan's family knew about her vibrant faith, but they were comfortable with a much more traditional and quiet expression of Christianity. Although prayer was part of their lives, I was concerned that this direct "listening-and-doing-what-the-Father-is-doing" style of prayer ministry might seem very strange. "Should we go pray for healing?" The thought intruded on our conversation but I batted it away. We offered comfort but we stopped before asking if we could pray. Somehow it didn't seem like an option.

Days later, the thought was still lurking. I could not stop thinking about healing. Despite acting timid on the outside, my heart was developing a raging case of faith. It was Thursday evening when I finally said something. "Do you think we should go pray for Susan's sister," I mused to my husband, not expecting much of an answer.

"Not unless they ask us to," he demurred.

"Are you sure, honey? I think we're supposed to offer to pray." That was about as far as my timidity would let me go.

"No, we should wait and see," he insisted. "Susan knows we're here. They can call if they want to."

That was clearly the end of it. There was nothing else I could say. I shook my head and resigned myself to a long wait.

The wait lasted perhaps two seconds. Almost before Phil finished speaking, the phone next to me rang. We looked at each other, too startled to know what to say. "Well, pick up the phone!" Phil prodded.

"Wendy?" It was Susan. Why was I not surprised? "My sister does have hepatitis and my mother's worried about her and about the wedding and, well, would you and Phil come over and pray?" This was starting to sound more and more like a setup.

"When's good?" I responded.

"Any time," she said. "She's jaundiced. And in bed. She's not exactly going anywhere."

Good point.

"How 'bout Saturday afternoon?" That would give me a day to intercede. I had no idea about what to do with hepatitis.

My pent-up faith came out in a rush. *Yay! We get to pray!* I was about to start jumping around the kitchen.

Then it left. Immediately. Totally. Every ounce of faith I had completely evaporated in about five nano-seconds.

Pray? What would happen when we prayed? What if nothing happened when we prayed? What if we just looked completely stupid when we prayed? What if it made it look like Jesus didn't still heal? Whose great idea was this, anyway?

But something strange was going on. Phil, who had been more than reluctant to do anything outside of the church sanctuary or our small group, was suddenly excited. All of my faith, it seemed, had exited my body and landed squarely in his lap.

"I like this" he exulted, "This will be great!"

Great. Yeah. Not what I was thinking. Mortifying, perhaps. Humiliating, certainly. But great? Suddenly, I was not looking forward to Saturday.

Phil, on the other hand, was humming, puttering, and feeling pretty good about life.

Saturday morning, I crawled out of bed with all the optimism of a soldier facing D-Day. Lovely. *Let's get this over,* I thought. I had absolutely no desire to pray.

Susan walked us into her sister's room and motioned vaguely to the side. I glanced at the bed, not knowing what to expect. Her sister certainly looked jaundiced. She was noticeably yellow.

Susan's mom looked hopefully at Phil and me. I was beginning to feel nauseous. She thought we knew what we were doing. *How quickly could we do this?*

I sat on the side of the bed, laid my hand on Susan's sister, and asked the Holy Spirit to come. All I could think of was how stupid we would look, and how disappointed they would be if this hepatitis-ridden patient didn't rise up and walk. And what would poor Susan go through, trying to defend Jesus and His ability to heal?

I tried to listen to the Lord. I hoped Phil would hear something. Finally, with zero faith I did the only thing I could do, the only thing that came to mind: I did everything I had ever been taught. I cursed the illness and I spoke health to her body and strength to her immune system.

Phil prayed briefly but I was too nervous to hear. Nothing was happening, the sister looked as sick as ever, and my romantic illusions of what healing would look like were dead. Pray for healing? Never again. Not in my lifetime. Someone said amen and we made a dash for the door.

Our church held prayer meetings on Sundays that summer and I spent the entire next day screaming silently at God who had gotten us into this. *You told us to pray,* I ranted. *So when do we see this stuff? When does healing happen? Why did you make us do that?* I wasn't shy about venting my feelings to my Father. *We did what you told us. Now why isn't something happening?* I knew all the answers but my heart exploded with the passion of unmet expectations. *When, God, WHEN?* If anyone had heard my inner tantrum they would have had me committed.

The day went by slowly. I hoped the phone would ring. Perhaps she was healed and we didn't know it. Not likely. I don't think I slept well; my rants continued. By Monday afternoon, I was trying hard to move on. My long obedience in one direction[19] had worn thin.

I was surprised when Susan called. Wedding plans, she was talking wedding plans. I was distracted. Until I heard the next sentence. "You do know what happened to my sister, don't you?" No, I didn't know what had happened to her sister and I was sure at this point that I didn't want to know. After all, she hadn't been healed.

"You mean they didn't tell you, they didn't *call you?* It's gone! The hepatitis is gone!"

It was *what?*

"She went to the doctor's this morning and the new tests came back normal. They thought they'd read the other results wrong but my sister told them, 'No, the test results weren't wrong. Jesus healed me!' My sister knew that Jesus healed her!"

Susan wasn't kidding. I was listening.

"My mother went running up and down the halls at work, yelling 'Jesus healed my daughter! Jesus healed my daughter!'" *Oh my. Oh my, oh my, oh my. God heard us? He listened? He healed her sister? And the whole family knew it was the Lord?*

---

[19] With apologies to Eugene Peterson for the allusion to his excellent title *A Long Obedience in the Same Direction.*

Susan's mother later told us her daughter's healing had changed their family forever but we didn't hear until years later what happened the day we prayed. Susan's sister had dreamt about her illness that night. In her dream, she saw the hepatitis cells, large and round and nasty looking. Then she saw her antibodies rising up, strong and healthy, shooting the hepatitis cells and killing them. I'd spoken strength to her immune system, strength to her body to fight off this infection.

Whatever our "normal" had been in the past, it had definitely just changed. The whole world was apparently the Holy Spirit's playground. We prayed for people every chance we got. God was at work; we just hadn't seen it before.

My timidity didn't entirely go away. We still missed many good opportunities and grieved about them later, but we were bolder now and we certainly wanted to "go into all the world."

We prayed in the Ukraine. We prayed in Mexico. We prayed in Kenya. We learned about inner healing. We trained students. We started a ministry. We taught. We wrote books. We lectured in Peru. Through it all, we never stopped listening. "Holy Spirit, come. Show us what you're doing."

Even through the dry seasons, we never stopped believing that "doing the stuff" was for every single believer, equipping the saints for the work of ministry.

To every generation...

Fast forward ten years. We had another small group, another generation to teach about healing, but our small group was changing.

We'd taught inner healing. We'd prayed small and large prayers and we'd listened intently. But this was different. A heart for "more" was emerging and that "more" was pointing to the world.

One by one, our small group members were pulled into missions. Their experiences were about to change their world, and ours.

Anne was timid when we first met her. She came to our teaching series and courageously kept coming even when the process seriously threatened her boundaries; being prayed for in front of the class was about the last straw. I was amazed when she wanted to join our small group. She was growing, fast.

Slowly, Anne began to see pictures from the Lord. Then she learned to pray what she saw. A teacher at heart, she always knew what the pictures meant and how they applied. Soon her natural feisty boldness, hidden for years under a wall of protection, gradually reappeared. Healing was good and it helped her incredibly, but listening was better and she was amazed as she saw God use her.

One night during the summer, a few of us gathered in our family room. Worship took us deeply into God's presence and when we re-emerged, God was obviously still at work. Anne sat quietly, trying to compose herself and to keep from shaking. She mentioned a mission trip; was she perhaps supposed to go? Knowing *our* answer (but not wanting to give advice), we just laughed and prayed more, wondering if something big was at hand. The Lord was calling her to something larger than her teaching job.

We prayed for another half-hour, with many revelations, but we remembered one word: Missions, missions, missions, missions—did I mention missions?

Anne volunteered for the mission trip and began to raise funds.

The Lord must have decided that this was Anne's year. One astounding event after another reverberated through her family. Wounds from the past surfaced. God healed traumas and pains. She finished raising support a full four months early and raised $750 more than she needed. Every few months we'd pray again for anointing and equipping. The Spirit was apparently not yet finished.

As the trip loomed closer, the enemy's attacks loomed larger. Anne was remarkably undeterred. She continued to ask for prayer for more of the Spirit's power; He invariably poured Himself out more and more and she spoke out more and more in prayer.

Before long, she was co-leading the prayer team for the trip and teaching others what she'd learned: Listen to God. Do what you hear. Minister rather than intercede. Take authority.

One night, not long before Anne's trip, a friend and I stayed after our group meeting to pray for her. We both knew that Anne was flying to a country rife with spiritual oppression. She would need all of the spiritual weapons she could gather. We prayed for power, gifts, discernment, authority, faith, wisdom, and anything else we could think of. We figured that if God wanted to give gifts, Anne could certainly use them for encouragement, authority, and warfare.

We prayed, the Holy Spirit's presence gently came over us, Anne shook… and nothing discernable happened. We weren't bothered since her reaction wasn't important; God's equipping was. The trip would necessitate a major worldview shift for Anne and we knew she was being prepared. We sent her off on her journey, waited, and prayed.

Early reports were encouraging: the trip was amazing. The team had bonded, the Holy Spirit had worked mightily to heal and to draw people to Jesus, and the hearts of the team were left with the people for whom they'd prayed.

But the biggest testimony didn't come until later, when we received an email from Anne. After twenty-plus years we didn't think we'd be shocked but what we read wasn't what we expected to hear.

Anne's email:

What is most pressing for me to tell you is that every prayer that was spoken over me before we left came to its *full fruition* in God. Every single one - even the releasing of the gifts of the spirit. (Yup, that's right - oh it occurred and every team member was there to witness it - I could have levitated it was so powerful.) It was the "Joy of the Lord" being released out to the group.

I was shaking as my physical body encountered a spiritual realm I'd never experienced before... I realized mid-prayer that I was worshiping with the angels surrounding Jesus as he sits on his throne. I saw Jesus desiring to walk into our midst... AND HE DID!!! That was confirmed at breakfast when a man in our group said he actually saw Jesus walk amongst us during the prayer. I smiled and felt confirmed that this day was only beginning...

Then there was the releasing of signs and wonders. That day and the next, every person who touched me, or whom I touched (while I was encountering Jesus), either witnessed or experienced miracles as the Lord worked through them. One person had 40 people stand up for Christ in a group immediately that afternoon. Another person saw a complete healing of a man's infected mouth - his mouth had been so infected that he could barely talk. He jumped up and shouted, "Alleluia!" (By the way, prayer for him took less than 5 minutes!) I saw a blind man see his own photograph, and I had a woman renounce her use of voodoo and serving two gods. A mother was completely healed of cancer.

I am feeling incredibly humbled, amazed and wowed by the Lord's use of me to begin something that great...

And so one timid evangelical teacher found herself changed by the power of the Spirit, mightily used by God, hearing His voice and courageously following Him even to the ends of the earth.

One week later, another group member went to a Power Evangelism conference and was healed of chronic neck and shoulder pain that had limited his activity for years. Then his wife and a friend prayed for a young woman and watched her lifelong skeletal problem disappear as they prayed.

We listen to God and we "do what the Father is doing." He's always moving, always equipping, always sending. It's new for every generation.

Toto? We're definitely not in Kansas any more. And I don't want to go home.

Chapter Twenty-One
Where Do We Go From Here?

It's a journey, this John-Five-Nineteen process. Listening and doing, risking and speaking, giving and receiving. Just when we think we've arrived, another challenge emerges in front of us, pulling us on.

As you have listened to Jesus, have you heard a new challenge? Have you caught a new vision? Has the way you have avoided suddenly become a calling? The nest we've been raised in becomes strangely prickly as the Father gently pushes us onto the edge. "Jump," He seems to say, "You will not fall! You will fly!"

For some of us, "Jump," means beginning to listen, beginning to risk in a brave new world, encountering a Jesus who we never knew could speak. What happens when we dare to hear intuitively? What happens when we speak what we hear? What if what we hear really is from God?

For others, "Jump," means surrendering to His will, His way, and the Holy Spirit's power. What happens when God's power is at work in us? What happens when we're no longer in control? Will we lose ourselves when the Spirit says, "Go?" What happens to the life we've known?

For some of us, "Jump," means changing the way we pray, taking the bold step of praying in an active voice, speaking to things with God's authority to speak. What happens when there is healing as we speak with God's voice?

For some, "Jump," means taking a radical step: to go out on the street and pray in the public arena, as Jesus did. What will happen when we listen for God's voice and "do what we see the

Father doing" on the street, in the market, and see miracles happen? Will that have an impact on the people we meet?

For some of us, "Jump," means taking off a mask of perfection, being strong enough to admit that we're weak and humble enough to say we need prayer. Do our communities grow when hurting people discover that it's safe to be real? Do we lose our standing in the eyes of others or gain it? What happens to our relationship with God?

For some, "Jump," means being quiet when we'd really rather speak. It means learning to give space and time and freedom to fail instead of advice and counsel. What happens if my counsel is no longer needed as I pray for others? Will they listen more, or less? Will sin abound more because my opinions were not shared? Or will grace open a different way of hearing and living?

And for some of us, "Jump," means digging deep into the pain we have buried, letting it rise and be healed instead of hiding it away. For those of us who risk this challenging journey, the forest is deep but the view from the clearing on the other side is amazing. What will happen when we find roots that have grown into a forest? Will we ever arrive at the clearing? What does real freedom look like?[20]

No matter which way we choose, the risk is daunting but the journey and the reward are worth pushing through our fear. The questions don't go away but they change and the answers are deeper and more satisfying. The way ahead provides hope because our God is a God who leads, guides, and speaks. He will not leave us where we are, to stagnate and fall behind. Nor

---

[20] For those of us who need to unveil our pain and find the roots that have caused us to stumble, the next book in this series continues our journey. It looks at the roots of the dysfunctions in our lives, and helps both pray-ers and seekers alike to uncover roots and untangle feet.

will He push us so far that we fall aside. He will speak. He will empower and equip us to do everything He has for us to do.

The next step may be a big one, but the Lord reminds us that where He leads us we will not fall. After all, we didn't launch ourselves into this venture. He called us. And when He calls, He sustains—and we fly.

> "For I know the plans I have for you," declares the LORD, "plans to prosper you and not to harm you, plans to give you hope and a future." (Jeremiah 29:11)

> "Being confident of this, that he who began a good work in you will carry it on to completion until the day of Christ Jesus." (Philippians 1:6)

He is faithful. He is able. He is ready. Are we?

Acknowledgments

We are indebted to John Wimber for his foundational teaching on the Kingdom of God and "Doing the Stuff." Without his conferences, seminars, books, tapes, and well-trained pastors, we would never have discovered prayer ministry. His commitment to empowering and equipping the laity and enabling them to empower and equip others launched us into a world we never knew existed. Together with books and teachings by Doug Gregg, Mike Flynn, Gary Wiens, and countless Vineyard pastors who loved "doing the stuff," John Wimber's material has formed a foundation for our teaching which has endured for the past 25 years.

There's a special place in our heart for those of you with whom this journey started. To Bill and Lainie Elander, Joe Paskewich and Bob Branch: you started something and nurtured it, and you have no idea how much you have impacted us and thousands of others. We can't thank you, and God, enough.

Thank you, too, to Charles, Heather, Meg, Mike, and the multitudes of friends who contributed stories, prayed, supported, edited, read, and walked with us as this book was written and prepared. We quite literally would not have finished this journey without you.

And to you who are reading now: bless you. Thank you for following our journey and for persevering in your own. It is an adventure you will never regret. May you know His abundant provision as you step out in faith, His clear voice as you listen, and His incredible anointing as you pray.

We are so grateful for all of you and for Him.

Wendy and Phil Coy

Exercises,
Guidelines
and Prayers

Appendix A
Getting Practical:
Exercises in Journaling
and Dialogue with God

> But when he, the Spirit of truth, comes, He will guide you into all truth. He will not speak on his own; he will speak only what he hears, and he will tell you what is yet to come, he will bring glory to me by taking from what is mine and making it known to you. (John 16:12-14)

Jesus longs to speak His love to us! There are many ways that He can do that, and many ways for us to encounter Him.

Look through the eleven exercises on the next pages. Find one that speaks to your heart and enables you to hear your Father's voice. Listen to His still small voice and write down what you hear.

His voice is usually not loud; it is quiet and leads us through intuition. As my friend Mike Flynn reminds us, God's voice is not heard through concentration; concentration will shut down our very ability to hear. Rather, it is heard through relaxing, focusing on the Lord, and paying attention to our minds, emotions and bodies.[21] Very small thoughts may become very big revelations. If such a thought floats across your mind, think about it and follow it. It may be the Holy Spirit, especially if it glorifies Jesus, speaks of loving Him more, or expresses His heart. It probably is Jesus!

---

[21] Concept from Mike Flynn, *A Course in Healing*, Fresh Wind, 2005. Used by permission

As in all things, we must be sure to stay within the broad boundaries of God's Word. For most of us, the words we hear will line up well with our knowledge of Jesus in Scripture[22]. His love is wide and deep, and He wants us to hear His kind words toward us.

How does it feel to hear words of love from your Father? Does it reassure you to know He is deeply concerned about you and the things that matter to you? Begin a dialogue with Him! So often we listen and hear only a tidbit from Him when He is longing to have a conversation. Try answering and talking with Him—you may discover you are in a dialogue with the Living God. He is not far off!

---

[22] If anything you hear is "off" from Scripture, then put that part aside. If you consistently hear things that seem to be unlike what you read in Scripture, you might want to find a trusted leader or friend to share your words with. Then spend time in the Psalms or the Gospels, and become familiar with God's heart. Scripture is always a trusted source for hearing the Lord's voice!

1. Write a Letter to God

Using just one side of one sheet of paper, write a letter to God, pouring out your heart to Him. Tell him how you feel—all of it! Are you anxious or afraid? What is upsetting you? Are you ashamed of something? Guilty? Hiding? Tell him that, too. What are your dreams? What are you desperately hoping for? What do you love about Him? How do you need Him to intervene? What do you hope He will do? Most importantly, empty out the hidden places of your heart to your loving Father—but just use one side of the page.

Then, on the other side, write God's answer to you. Don't think too hard about this—if you're concentrating hard on what to write, you may actually block out His still small voice. What is your first impression of what He is saying? Write it down... And you may find yourself writing more. What is the Father saying back to you? If it sounds helpful, loving and gracious, it's probably God!

2. Meditation on Scripture

Choose a short Scripture that seems to resonate with your heart or mind. It may be one you love, one you've memorized, one you want to learn more about, or a new one you find in this list. Any Scripture which impacts your heart is fine. Read it once, quickly. Then go back and reread it slowly, pausing to think about the phrases which "jump out" at you. What is the Lord saying through these phrases? What new meaning do they have today? How do they answer the cry of your heart? What does this verse remind you about God? As thoughts occur to you, write them down on one of the following blank pages. As you write down what you are thinking, consider what God is telling you. Write down the thoughts you hear from Him.

Scriptures to use if you need to hear something new from the Lord:

Ps. 139:1-17
Eph. 1:15-23
1 Cor. 2:11-16
Col. 3:12-17
John 15:9-17
Is. 49:13-16
Jer. 29:11
Is. 61:1-6
Ps. 86:1-8

3. Write a Psalm to God

David's Psalms are heart cries to God. They extol God, worship God, beg God, bargain with God, and express frustration. But above all they are prayers that reflect on the relationship between God and people, and on God's ways and works among the people. Try writing your own psalm to God. It can express frustration, praise, hope, fear or whatever your heart wishes to express to God. Listen for His response and assurance even as (or after) you write. Include anything about which He answers or assures you. If possible, end with thanks and praise for who God is and/or what He has done.

Need help? Choose a psalm to read as an example. If you're stuck, try Psalm 5, Psalm 8, Psalm 27, Psalm 30; Psalm 130; Psalm 138.

4. Sing to the Lord a New Song

Find a quiet place where you will not disturb anyone else. Ask God to speak to your heart. Sing to God a worship song that comes to mind. Listen to the words and meditate on their meaning and God's response. Is God saying something to you through the song? Do the words have any special meaning to you? Are the words part of a Scripture verse?

Or try making up a song to God and singing that—don't worry about the structure, but sing what comes to mind.

Later, write down what you learn.

If a song doesn't come to mind now, make a mental note as you wake up tomorrow, or as you go about the tasks of your day. If you realize there is a song in the background of your mind, make note of it. Are the words something that God is saying to your heart? What do they mean to you?

5. Take a Walk with God

Take a walk outside with Jesus. Imagine He is there with you, walking and talking. Talk to Him as if He was REALLY there (you may do it out loud, but it's probably better to do that only if you're alone—although you could try wearing a wireless earbud or headset and pray that passersby will think you're on the phone). Listen to His responses. Or just walk and look at the world around you, telling him in your heart how it makes you feel. Sometimes try walking in silence with him – good friends don't always need words to "be together."

Then, write down what you learned, felt or heard from God.

6. Silence with Jesus

Imagine taking each of your worries, burdens, and cares carefully into your hands, then placing each in a box and giving the box to Jesus (read Philippians 4:6-7). Sit quietly and ask the Holy Spirit to come and fill the place where those worries and burdens have been. Ask Him to speak to you there. Pay attention to Him as He does that, and see what He says to you. Note anything that you see or hear (or think, in your heart or mind), especially when you give Him your box. Write down what seems important.

7. Purify My Heart

God works to change us from inside our hearts. Take some time to pray and ask God to purify your heart and mind by the work of His Spirit. The key to this prayer is your willingness to completely surrender the control of your life to God. Ask Him to search your heart and see if there is anything He wants to purify or change, or if there is anything He would have you do differently or stop doing. Then listen for Him to tell you or incline your heart. When you sense what He is saying, ask the Holy Spirit to cleanse you from that sin and take away even the desire for it. Ask Him to fill that place with his holiness and the strength of the Spirit. Write down what you learn.[23]

---

[23] Adapted from A Spiritual Formation Workbook, Small Group Resources for Nurturing Christian Growth, by James Bryan Smith. Harper San Francisco1991, 1993, p. 29.

8. A Devotional Time

Find a devotional reading (if you don't have one, Oswald Chambers' *My Utmost For His Highest, Upper Room,* or some other devotional will do). Choose a selection and read it as if God was in the room, sitting next to you. Respond to it and see if you can discover what He is saying to you. If you prefer, use one of the selections on this page and the next.[24]

Intimate Theology "Do You Believe This?"-John 11:26

Martha believed in the power available to Jesus Christ; she believed that if He had been there He could have healed her brother; she also believed that Jesus had a special intimacy with God, and that whatever He asked of God, God would do. But – she needed a closer personal intimacy with Jesus. Martha's theology had its fulfillment in the future. But Jesus continued to attract and draw her in until her belief became and intimate possession. It then slowly emerged into a personal inheritance – "Yes, Lord, I believe that You are the Christ... (11:27)

Is the Lord dealing with you in the same way? Is Jesus teaching you to have a personal intimacy with Himself? Allow Him to drive His question home to you – "Do you believe this?" Are you facing an area of doubt in your life? Have you come, like Martha, to a crossroads of overwhelming circumstances where your theology is about to become a very personal belief? This happens only when a personal problem brings the awareness of our personal need.

To believe is to commit. In the area of intellectual learning I commit myself mentally, and reject anything not related to that belief. In the realm of personal belief I commit myself morally to my convictions and refuse to compromise. But in intimate personal belief I commit myself spiritually to Jesus Christ and make a determination to be dominated by Him alone.

Then, when I stand face to face with Jesus Christ and He says to me, "Do you believe this?" I find that faith is as natural as breathing. And I am staggered when I think how foolish I have been in not trusting Him earlier[25]

---

[24] Ibid., p.23.

[25] November 6 reading from *My Utmost For His Highest,* by Oswald Chambers, © 1935 Dodd, Mead & Co., © renewed 1963 Oswald Chambers Publications Association Ltd., © 1995 Oswald Chambers Publications Association Ltd.

Maintaining the Proper Relationship
"The Friend of the Bridegroom?" - John 3:29

Goodness and purity should never be traits that draw attention to themselves. But should simply be magnets that draw people to Jesus Christ. If my holiness is not drawing others to Him, it is not the right kind of holiness; it is only an influence which awakens undue emotions and evil desires in people and diverts them from heading in the right direction. A person who is a beautiful saint can be a hindrance in leading people to the Lord by presenting only what Christ has done for him, instead of presenting Jesus Christ Himself. Others will be left with this thought – "What a fine person that man is!" That is not being a true "friend of the bridegroom" – *I* am increasing al the time; *He* is not.

To maintain this friendship and faithfulness to the Bridegroom, we have to be more careful to have the moral and vital relationship to Him above everything else, including obedience. Sometimes there is nothing to obey and our only task is to maintain a vital connection with Jesus Christ, seeing that nothing interferes with it. Only occasionally is it a matter of obedience. At those times when a crisis arises, we have to find out what God's will is. Yet most of our life is not spent in trying to be consciously obedient, but in maintaining this relationship – being the "friend of the bridegroom." Christian work can actually be a means of diverting a person's focus away from Jesus Christ. Instead of being friends "of the bridegroom," we may become amateur providences of God to someone else, working against Him while we use His weapons.[26]

---

[26] Ibid., March 25 reading.

9. Yielding to the Work of the Spirit

Spend some time specifically asking for the Holy Spirit to begin working in your life in a new and powerful way. Seek the Lord and tell Him the desires of your heart for Him. Neither demand nor expect, but surrender yourself to Him. Spend time worshipping Jesus and telling Him of your love for Him. Ask Him to fill any holes or needful places in your life.

If you wish to, concentrate on either the fruit (Galatians 5:22) or the gifts of the Spirit (many places, but try I Corinthians 12:8-11). If you desire to, ask Him to point out any gifts He wants to impart to you or develop in you. Ask Him to renew any latent or neglected gifts (see 1 Timothy 4:4). Seek Him for any gifts you particularly desire. Ask Him to fill the desires of your heart for Him. Spend time expressing your love to Him and listen for Him to express His heart to you.[27]

Later, write down anything you learn or hear from Him.

---

[27] Smith, op cit., pp. 37-38

10. An Exercise in Service, Blessing and Intercession

Ask God to reveal to you anyone you know whom He would like to bless through you. Spend a moment and write a very brief note to those one or two people. Thank them for something meaningful they have done. Bless them for their service to you, or God, or write whatever God tells you to write to bless them. Include any Scripture verses that seem appropriate, especially if a particular verse comes to mind while you are thinking of them. Spend time asking God to bless them and fill their life with His Spirit. Ask Him if there is anything you can do to bless them and lead them closer in their walk with Jesus. Listen for His answer.

Write down anything you learn.

Then focus on Jesus and ask Him to show you how HE would be blessing YOU in the same way. Imagine that HE wrote a note to YOU blessing you in your relationship to Him. Pray about that and see if He says anything to YOU.

11. A Missions Moment

Ask God through His Holy Spirit to impress a nation or region of the world on your mind or heart. Take a few moments in silence and mentally survey the world map, or imagine the countries in your mind. Does a particular region come to mind or seem particularly important to you? Do you have a strong desire to pray for one area? Ask God to show you what to pray for that place. Pray what seems important and ask for God's reviving and saving work in that region.

Ask for His heart for the people there and ask if there is anything you can do to participate in His work there – write to a missionary, pray for the people, do a short missions trip, send money, work on a project, etc. Write down anything you learn or hear from Him.

Later, research that country in a mission's handbook such as "Operation World" and see what other needs you can pray for in that region.

Appendix B
Listening Prayer Exercise

Objective: To give participants the chance to listen and pray for one another in a safe environment and receive feedback.

Directions:

- Divide group up into smaller groups of 3 or 4 at most.
- Pick someone as designated "leader."
- The person to the leader's left will receive prayer first.
- Leader asks permission to lay hands on the person receiving prayer.
- Leader prays to open: ask the Holy Spirit to come, show how to pray (Permission and prayer, max 30 seconds.)
- Without any discussion, everyone listens to God for what to pray. (Allow listening for max of 2 minutes.)
- Pray: Everyone prays only what they saw or heard. (2 minutes)
- Debrief: Pray-ee gives feedback about whether what was prayed was right, connected, or made sense; and what he or she really needs prayer for. (max 2-3 minutes)
- All: Based on what was shared, pray again for the person. (max 2-3 minutes)
- Leader: Pray to seal what God has done and close. (30 seconds)
- Rotate around the circle. The person who just received prayer becomes the next leader. The pray-ee is on the leader's left.
- After everyone has had a chance to listen, pray, and be prayed for, ask how many had people pray for them things which had to be God? How many heard God sensed His direction in new ways, or for first time?

> Note: The whole process should not take more than 10 minutes per person. Be ruthless or it will go all night!

Listening prayer exercise original source: Doug Gregg, Arcadia CA. Presented at IVCF Prayer Retreat, Connecticut, September 1991. Unpublished notes. Revised and updated by Phil and Wendy Coy (innerACTS), 1997-2009

Appendix C
Guidelines for a Healthy and Productive Prayer Session

Do:

1. Remember that you represent Jesus. Even when you do not intend to, you model Jesus to the person you pray for. Your two objectives in any ministry situation are to glorify God and to love the person.

2. "Dial down." Wait on the Lord for what to do. Listen more, talk less.

3. Ask the person's permission to: touch them, pray with them, or do anything that involves them.

4. Keep your eyes open. Ask them to close their eyes and focus on the Lord.

5. Keep ministry private so as not to draw attention to yourself or the situation.

6. Keep everything that happens confidential.

7. Remember, God can and will do what is needed. You only need to ask.

8. Always engage and minister to a person with love and respect, and guard his or her dignity.

9. Discuss follow-up: What are the next steps after prayer?

10. If you doubt the person knows Jesus, inquire gently. If they don't, consider briefly sharing with them and asking if they'd like to know the Lord.

11. If anything weird, hard, or unusual happens, involve other more experienced team members. You don't need to know how to handle every situation.

Don't:

1. Don't counsel. You are not there to counsel, but to ask and seek God's help. Avoid giving advice.

2. Don't project your own problems onto the person you are praying for.

3. Don't do more than the Lord is doing. Sometimes God will have you do little, sometimes much. Trust Him to know the pace at which things should go.

4. Don't dominate in a prayer time when there are others praying alongside. Keep you prayer concise and allow others to contribute.

5. You do not have to finish everything in one session! If you consistently hit a "roadblock" or the person is unable to receive, either pray for the presence of the Lord and bless what He is doing, or gently close the ministry session. Suggest further in-depth prayer at another time, or refer to another prayer person.

6. Don't pray alone unless you absolutely have to. Prayer team members provide protection, support, intercession... and training opportunities.

7. Do nothing for hype, effect, control or manipulation. We are committed to honesty and integrity.

Appendix D
The Interview Healing Prayer Model

Before you begin, explain the guidelines for prayer, including confidentiality.

1) Interview

❖ Ask, "Where does it hurt?" or "How long have you had it?" or "What do you want the Lord to do?" Look for the root of the condition.

❖ Listen both to the person and to God. Don't try to provide the rational answer or give advice. Keep it brief.

2) Diagnosis

❖ Why does the person have the problem?

❖ Look for spiritual, generational and sinful root patterns

❖ Common causes and roots:

o Sin
o Emotional stress
o Rejection
o Neglect / Abandonment
o Abuse
o Control
o Demonic spirits

o Anger
o Unforgiveness
o Virus
o Accident
o Trauma
o Generational patterns
o Use of Magic /occult

3) Prayer Selection

❖ What kind of prayer will help?

❖ Common kinds of prayer:

o Petition—asking for the Holy Spirit's guidance, presence and healing

o Intercession—asking God to help the person

o Command of faith—speaking to the condition

o Forgiveness—giving or receiving forgiveness

o Deliverance—binding or expelling spirit(s) causing the condition

- o   Pronouncement – e.g. "You are healed"

4) Invite the Holy Spirit to Come, Pray —and "Check In"

- ❖   Tell the person to relax, not to pray unless they are strongly led to, or unless you ask.
- ❖   Ask the Holy Spirit to come, and wait for His presence to be manifested or for Him to show you how to pray.
- ❖   Pray!
- ❖   Keep checking in with the person to see what's happening.
- ❖   Pray again in accordance with their report.
- ❖   Stop praying when:
  - o   The person says it's over or looks up and stops receiving.
  - o   God says it's over.
  - o   You can't think of anything else to do, nor can anyone else.
  - o   You've prayed for everything but there's no progress.
  - o   You're out of time.

5) Post-Prayer

- ❖   What does the person need to do to continue on?
- ❖   Alert the person to the possibility of counter-attack— symptoms and thoughts may appear in the next day or two that suggest he or she has not been healed. The person may need to willfully rebuke those thoughts for a few moments.
- ❖   If appropriate, encourage the person to make decisions and take actions that will help.

Portions of this interview prayer model taken from Mike Flynn, *A Course in Healing*. Fresh Wind, 2005. www.freshwindministries.org

Appendix E
Prayers for Protection and Cleansing

Prayer For Protection

(before ministry, from Francis MacNutt)

In the name of Jesus Christ, and by the power of his Cross and his Blood, we bind up the power of any evil spirits and command them not to block our prayers. We bind up the power of earth, air, water, fire, the netherworld and the satanic forces of nature.

We break any curses, hexes, or spells sent against us and declare them null and void. We break the assignments of any spirits sent against us and send them to Jesus to deal with them as He will. Lord, we ask you to bless our enemies by sending your Holy Spirit to lead them to repentance and conversion.

Furthermore, we bind all interaction and communication in the world of spirits as it affects us and our ministry.

We ask for the protection of the shed blood of Jesus Christ over _____ (insert name)

Thank you Lord, for your protection and send your angels to help us in the battle. We ask you to guide us in our prayers; share with us your Spirit's power and compassion. Amen.

Prayer To Be Set Free

(following ministry, from Francis MacNutt)

Lord Jesus, thank you for sharing with us your wonderful ministry of healing and deliverance. Thank you for the healings we have seen and experienced today.

We realize that the sickness and evil we encounter is more than our humanity can bear. So cleanse us of any sadness, negativity or despair that we may have picked up.

If our ministry has tempted us to anger, impatience or lust, cleanse us of those temptations and replace them with love, joy and peace.

If any evil spirits have attached themselves to us or oppressed us in any way, we command you, spirits of earth, air, fire or water, of the netherworld or of nature, to depart – now – and go straight to Jesus Christ for Him to deal with them as he will.

Come Holy Spirit, renew us, fill us anew with your power, your life and your joy. Strengthen us where we have felt weak and clothe us with your light. Fill us with life.

And Lord Jesus, please send your holy angels to minister to us and our families – guard us and protect us from all sickness, harm and accidents. Gives us a safe trip home.

We praise you now and forever, Father, Son and Holy Spirit, and we ask these things in Jesus' Holy Name that He may be glorified. Amen.

Protection Prayers

(from Mike Flynn)

I sign myself with the sign of the cross. I cover myself with the Blood of the Lamb. I surround myself with the Light of the Cross and in the Name of Jesus Christ, nothing shall come through to hurt me.

(Then pray this over any special needs, individuals, or circumstances.)

I assert now that I and those I've prayed for are fully protected in body, soul, and spirit, in mind, will and emotions, in circumstance, relationships and finance, and against all assaults of the world, the flesh and the devil.

Prayer for Spiritual Armor

(from Mike Flynn)

Lord Jesus Christ, I greet you this morning as my commander and chief, reporting for duty. But first, I need to clothe myself with your armament, for my own is of no use against the enemy. Therefore I take to myself the belt of truth. I will desire, speak and act in accordance with the truth. Second, I take on the breastplate or righteousness. Thank you that this is your righteousness, and that it protects my vital organs, especially my heart. I will speak, think and act righteously. Third, I put on the shoes of the gospel of peace, and I will prepare that good news by reading your word and being ready to give an account for the hope that is in me. Fourth, I take on the helmet of salvation. Save me, Lord, from the world, the flesh, and the devil. And I will trust you to give me the mind of Christ and to think your thoughts in my mind. Next, I take the shield of faith by which to quench all the flaming arrows of the enemy – arrows of temptation, accusation, deception, and harassment. Finally, having seen to my defense, I take the sword, that particular word which the Spirit gives, to utter against Satan in whichever way You lead. Over it all Lord, I take the mantle of love, asking you to give me your love for all whom I encounter today. I decide by this that I am effectively armored for whatever spiritual warfare comes my way today.

Protection Prayers if You are Under Spiritual Attack
(from Mike Flynn)

In the name of Jesus Christ crucified, died and risen, I bind all spirits of the air, the atmosphere, the water, the fire, the wind, the ground, the underground, and the nether world. I also bind the influence of any lost or fallen soul who may be present, and all emissaries of the satanic headquarters or any coven or witches or warlocks or satan worshippers who may be present in some preternatural way. I claim the blood of Jesus on the air and atmosphere, the water, the fire, the wind, the ground and their fruits all around us, the underground and the nether world. In the name of Jesus Christ, I forbid every adversary mentioned to communicate with or help one another in any way or to communicate with me, except as I permit.

Lord I ask You to bless our enemies by sending your Holy Spirit to lead them to repentance. In the Name of Jesus Christ, I seal this place and all present and all family and associates of those present and their places and possessions and sources of supply in the blood of Jesus.

In the name of Jesus Christ, I forbid any lost souls, covens, satanic groups or emissaries or any of their associates, subjects or supervisors to harm or take revenge on me, my family, my associates, or cause harm or damage to anything we have.

In the name of Jesus Christ and by the merits of His precious blood, I break, decommission and dissolve every curse, hex, seal, spell, sorcery, bond, snare, trap, device, lie, stumbling block, obstacle, deception, diversion or distraction, spiritual chain or spiritual influence, every temptation, accusation or harassment, also every disease of body, soul, mind or spirit placed upon us, or on this place, or on any of the persons, places, and things mentioned, by any agent, or brought on us by our own mistakes or sins. Amen.

Bibliography

Chambers, Oswald. *My Utmost For His Highest*. © 1935 Dodd, Mead & Co., © renewed 1963 Oswald Chambers Publications Association Ltd., ©1995 Oswald Chambers Publications Association Ltd.

Flynn, Mike. *A Course in Healing*. Fresh Wind, 2005. www.freshwindministries.org

Flynn, Mike, and Doug Gregg. *Inner Healing*. Downers Grove, Illionois: InterVarsity Press, 1993.

Foster, Richard. *Celebration of Discipline*. San Francisco: Harper, 1988.

Jackson, John Paul. *Needless Casualties of War*. Streams Publications, 1999.

Kreider, Larry. *Hearing God 30 Different Ways*. House to House, 2005.

MacNutt, Francis. *Healing*. Notre Dame: Ave Maria Press, 1974, 1999.

Payne, Leanne. *Listening Prayer*. Grand Rapids: Baker, 1994.

Sheets, Dutch. *Intercessory Prayer*. Regal Books, 1996.

Simmons, Brian. *Song of Songs, the Journey of the Bride*. Insight Publishing, 2002.

Smith, James Bryan. *A Spiritual Formation Workbook*. San Francisco: Harper, 1993.

Virkler, Mark. *Dialogue with God*. Bridge Publishing, 1986.

Virkler, Mark and Patti. *How to Hear God's Voice*. Image Publishers, 2005.

Wiens, Gary. *Bridal Intercession, Authority in Prayer Through Intimacy With Jesus*. Oasis House, 2001.

Wimber, John. *Power Healing*. San Francisco: Harper Row, 1987. *Power Evangelism*. San Francisco: Harper Row, 1986.

Also by Ascribe Publishing

**Journey to the
Center of God's Heart**
By Charles Simpson

*Seeing Him through the eyes of
the Seers*

Come with me on a journey to
the real final frontier, the heart of
the Almighty God. The
discoveries along the way have
made this the most exciting
expedition I've ever been on.

As we see the Lord through the
eyes of the seers, we experience inward transformation that is
deep and permanent.

www.ascribepublishing.com

Also by Ascribe Publishing

Christian Island Parables
Humility, A Wholesome Tongue, and Contentment
by Charles Simpson

"In the Sea of Humanity, off the coast of Mammon, there's an island called Christian, where Mr. Saved Soul is the Mayor. Because of its beautiful beaches and abundant orchards, this island's reputation became much larger than its actual size."

Thus begins the first of three parables in which Mayor Saved Soul learns how to overcome pride, gossip, and discontentment. The setting is on Christian Island, a tranquil place where the Mayor serves under the care and authority of the great King. Although the following stories are intentionally light and friendly, don't be fooled! Their teachings are meant to be life-changing. The more we find ourselves relating to Mayor Saved Soul, the deeper we can appreciate and apply the lessons he learns.

 # *Resources from*
www.inneracts.org

innerACTS equips emerging leaders to minister effectively in prayer, worship and small groups, advancing the Kingdom of God by doing what the Father is doing.

Publications:

The Two-Talent Series: Practical Ministry for the Rest of Us

   Vol. 1:   *Learning to Pray Like Jesus: John Five Nineteen*

   Vol. 2:   *God's Healing from the Inside Out:*
            Getting to the Roots in Inner Healing Prayer
            (available January, 2010)

DVD Series: *God's Healing from the Inside Out*
            10-session DVD series including teachings and study guide for God's Healing from the Inside Out
            (available January, 2010)

Tough Stuff: 12 Comprehensive Lessons on Growing Through Life's Deepest Pains - curriculum for youth workers

SOULutions: relational healing for the next generation. Workbook for sexuality issues

Seminars and Retreats:

innerACTS offers seminars and retreats on prayer, listening prayer, prayer ministry, healing, inner healing, small groups, and ministry giftings.

Learning to Pray Like Jesus: a five-session weekend seminar equipping participants to hear from God and pray for one another using a framework for inner healing prayer.

God's Healing from the Inside Out: a ten-session series combining teaching, ministry, interaction and small groups to deal with the roots of issues and dysfunctional patterns in our lives, and to train leaders to address those issues with inner healing prayer.

Breinigsville, PA USA
05 April 2010
235540BV00004B/5/P